The Executive's Guide to Successful MRP II

The Executive's Guide to Successful MRP II

REVISED EDITION

Oliver W. Wight

John Wiley & Sons, Inc.
New York • Chichester • Brisbane • Toronto • Singapore

Contents

FOREWORD   vii

"WHY DIDN'T MRP II MAKE THE WALL STREET JOURNAL?"   ix

CHAPTER 1
WHY THE EXCITEMENT ABOUT MRP II TODAY?   1

CHAPTER 2
DOES MRP II APPLY TO MY BUSINESS?   11

CHAPTER 3
WHAT RESULTS CAN WE EXPECT?   19

CHAPTER 4
WHAT DOES MRP II COST?   29

CHAPTER 5
WHY SHOULD THE EXECUTIVE CARE?   39

CHAPTER 6
WHAT MUST BE DONE TO BE SUCCESSFUL WITH MRP II?   43

CHAPTER 7
HOW DO WE IMPLEMENT MRP II?   51

CHAPTER 8
HOW DO WE MANAGE WITH MRP II?   61

REFERENCES   71

THE IMPLEMENTATION PLAN   77

EXCERPTS FROM THE OLIVER WIGHT ABCD CHECKLIST   97
    INTRODUCTION   99
    HOW TO USE THE CHECKLIST   103
    PLANNING AND CONTROL PROCESSES   109

Foreword

We will, undoubtedly, look back on the 1980s as the decade of the new industrial revolution. We saw our radio industry, our television industry, and our small appliance industry invaded by the Japanese, and didn't pay much attention. But when they brought us to our knees in our own automobile industry, we suddenly realized that our claim to be number one in manufacturing was being challenged.

By 1980, articles and talks called for the "reindustrialization of America." Productivity became a pervasive theme.

Manufacturing Resource Planning (MRP II) had evolved, meanwhile, out of Material Requirements Planning (MRP) into a company game plan. And the successful users demonstrated that these tools could be used to raise the level of professionalism in running our manufacturing businesses dramatically.

This book is a brief guide for the executive who would like to know more about MRP and MRP II, or the executive who **has** been educated and would like a refresher. It is not, obviously, a substitute for a formal education experience; it is a **guide.**

It won't take that long to read it cover to cover, and I hope you will. But the book was intended, also, as a brief, handy **reference** for the executive. As the subject comes to mind, you can refer back to the appropriate chapter.

This book is written in **question and answer** format. The **questions are not contrived.** They are based on my **discussions with several thousand executives** every year at our classes, at talks, and while consulting. Their contributions to my thinking, as well as those of my closest associates: Dave Garwood, Walt Goddard, Darryl Landvater — and, of course, Joan — must be acknowledged.

The terms MRP (Material Requirements Planning), Closed Loop MRP, and MRP II (Manufacturing Resource Planning) are discussed in Chapter 1. Note that throughout the book where it isn't important to distinguish between them, the term MRP is used generically just for the sake of simplicity. Usually the meaning is conveyed by the content of the sentence, just as we speak of New York and sometimes mean Manhattan, all the boroughs of New York, or New York State, without specifically defining which we mean every time we use the term.

I sincerely hope this book helps you on your "MRP journey."

Oliver W. Wight
Blodgett Landing, NH
December, 1981

"Why Didn't MRP II Make the Wall Street Journal?"

OW   It does all the time.

Exec   Come on, Ollie. The Wall Street Journal never heard of MRP II—and if they did, they would probably think it was some kind of a computer system!

OW   But they **do** write about it. Didn't you read about the company that had to restate earnings because of an inventory shrinkage?

Exec   Which one? That happens all the time!

OW   How about our need for better productivity — or the fact that the Japanese work better as a team than we do?

Exec   I must say I'm getting a little tired of this Japanese stuff, but teamwork is something we sure could do better.

OW   Remember the company that took a long strike because their employees got sick of chronic overtime?

Exec   I know who you mean. They suffered terrible financial repercussions.

OW   How about the cash flow problem at the company that evidently didn't know how to gear production to sales and had to sell off their inventory at distress prices?

Exec   But the journal didn't mention MRP II in these articles, did they?

OW   No, they didn't. And when they talked about the performance at Black & Decker, Cameron Iron Works, Tennant Company and others that are Class A MRP II users, they didn't mention the credit their management gives to **having** these better tools either.

Exec   I hear your point, but why pick on the Wall Street Journal?

OW   Would you have preferred Forbes? Seriously, I'm just trying to illustrate the point that these business journals see what is on the surface, but they really don't understand much about cause and effect in a manufacturing enterprise. But that's what I wrote this book about. If you'll share a little of your valuable time with me, we can discuss the **real** problems and some of the tools for addressing them.

The Executive's Guide to Successful MRP II

Chapter 1

Why the Excitement About MRP II Today?

Exec   We've been exploding bills of material for years and doing "requirements planning," why all the excitement about material requirements planning—MRP—today?

OW   Because what was "requirements planning" developed into the tools to make valid **schedules.** Something we never had before! And once we solved the scheduling problem, we were able to have a company game plan that worked! A set of tools to enable management to control cash flow, inventories, labor and material purchases. Tools to support marketing better and provide far more useful financial information. Tools that enable companies to reduce inventories, improve customer service, and improve overall productivity.

Exec   But wait a minute. Wasn't MRP originally an inventory control technique?

OW   MRP, or as it was called, "requirements planning," was originally used as an **ordering** technique. One company I know, for example, calculated their material requirements through the bills of material once a month, four months into the future. Each month they would add a new month, but they **didn't recalculate the requirements** for months 1, 2, and 3. In fact, the books on inventory management, back in those days, said inventory management is concerned with "When to order," and "How much to order." Before the computer came along, ordering was all the inventory control people could do. They "order launched." When the computer came along, we used it to mechanize the ordering. It didn't occur to us to use it to do something completely different that couldn't be done before.

Exec   I've heard production and inventory control called a "push system and a pull system."

OW   That expresses it well. The **formal** inventory control system pushed orders into the plant and out to the vendors. This was true whether they used order point systems or requirements planning systems, the two basic methods for determining "When to order." But the original dates on the orders were bound to be wrong before long. Back in those days, we said: "If only we could have a forecast that is correct!", "If only the engineers wouldn't make changes!", "If only the machines wouldn't break down!" We tried to get the world to hold still, but the world of manufacturing wouldn't. It was a world of change, and the original dates that were placed on orders were soon wrong. That's where the "pull system" — the **informal** system — came into play. It was the shortage list generated from true demand; assembly requirements in a company making an assembled product, for example.

Exec   So the pull system became the real schedule, didn't it? Why couldn't we have used it without a push system?

OW   The problem was one of lead time. The lead time for planning. When we pull parts out of a stockroom, for example, to find out what the shortages are going to be, we're faced with a dilemma: If we pull them to meet the next three weeks' assembly requirements, for example, that doesn't tell us far enough in advance what the shortages are going to be; but if we pull them to cover the next **six weeks'** assembly requirements, we really don't know which parts we need first. The farther out we try to extend the horizon of the shortage list, the less we know what the true priority is.

Exec   Does MRP eliminate the push/pull system?

OW   It formalizes the pull system and eliminates the push system. MRP simulates the shortage list week by week (or day by day) and recalculates requirements weekly or daily by exception messages. The shortage list says: "What are we going to make, what does it take to make it, what do we have in inventory, what do we have to get?" With the material requirements plan, we put a master production schedule into the computer (what are we going to make), we put a bill of material into the computer (what does it take to make it), we put an inventory record into the computer (what do we have), and we generate material requirements (what do we have to get). MRP is a simulator that can push the planning horizon out as far into the future as we like, yet break the time increments for planning down fine enough so that we know what the relative priority of each item really is. And it can redo the simulation weekly, or even daily.

Exec   Why did it take so long to develop MRP? We've had commercially practical computers since the mid '50s, yet even today I understand that the companies that are really using MRP well are in the minority.

OW   We were learning to use tools we never had before. We were doing things we couldn't do before. By definition, then, we didn't know what these things were. It took a lot of time and experience on the part of the users to learn how to do it. The computer made it possible to do time phasing — breaking requirements down into finer time increments — as it became more powerful and had more file space economically available. About 1961, we started recognizing that rescheduling of material already on order was at least as important as knowing "when to order." By 1971, we recognized that the master production schedule (I'll call it "master schedule" for brevity) that drove the entire MRP system was the real key to simulating the shortage lists and having schedules that represented the real needs. But this was all user developed and all from trial and error.

Exec   That's interesting because I can't remember reading much about the master schedule before the early '70s. I don't believe I ever saw an example of a master schedule until a few years back.

OW   Right. In fact, a standard format for the master schedule is something that's come about only in the last four or five years. This standard format shows what the forecast demand is, what the actual demand is, what the master build schedule is, and what items in the master schedule are still "available to promise" in a make-to-order situation. The available to promise is uncommitted material and capacity available for incoming customer orders. Managing the master schedule is one of the most critical elements in making MRP work.

Exec   You talked about rescheduling material currently on order. Do you mean rescheduling material to a later date as well as moving it to an earlier date, i.e. expediting it?

OW   Absolutely. And this is an important message to get to people who have lived in order launching and expediting mode. The attitude often is, "Just because one component was scrapped and won't be in until three weeks later, I'm not about to take the pressure off the other components. I'll show them needed at the original due date, rather than reschedule. If I didn't, you can be sure that when the missing component came in I'd be missing something else!" In a world where schedules didn't mean very much, this attitude is understandable. Unfortunately, it's also self-defeating. You can't get material that you **don't** need without getting it instead of material that you **do** need.

The general manager of one company was ready to fire his purchasing agent because every time they went to make products, one or more purchased components were missing. But the problem wasn't really the fact that the purchasing agent wasn't putting in the effort. The fact of the matter was that the purchasing agent didn't know which of the "past due" items were really needed most and which ones to concentrate on getting in. There were many components that were past due that weren't needed, and a few that were past due that were needed. The first step was to give the purchasing agent a valid schedule so that he knew what was really needed.

Of course, the expeditor is only looking for the material that is needed. He sees that it is past due and blames purchasing for not having the material "in on time," not recognizing that there are plenty of other items that are past due that aren't really needed now. One of the most insidious by-products of the informal system is that it makes everyone's performance look bad, and everybody blames everybody else when things don't go right— which is most of the time!

Exec Lately I've heard about "Closed Loop MRP." Just what is that?

OW Once again, this was something that evolved from the application of material requirements planning in the real world. The elements of a Closed Loop MRP system are shown in Figure 1.

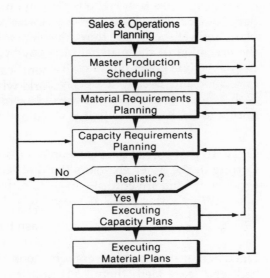

Figure 1. Closed Loop Diagram

It rapidly became obvious that the material requirements plan offered a powerful scheduling — or "priority planning" — capability. This is the "heart" of the closed loop system. But the material requirements plan had to be driven by a master schedule that identified the finished units in a make-to-stock business or the building blocks of assemblies or groups of components in a make-to-order business that were actually going to be made. This, in turn, was derived from the sales & operations plan which is a statement of the production rate (usually in units for a product family) like: "We are going to build 1500 'model thirty' pumps per week."

It became apparent too that if we couldn't plan the capacity requirements to meet the material requirements, the plan wasn't really valid. Here again, the fundamental manufacturing equation, "What are we going to make, what does it take to make it, what do we have, what do we have to get," is used, only this time it's in standard hours rather than units. Once the material and capacity requirements plans to execute a given sales & operations plan and master schedule have been developed, the question is whether or not these plans are realistic — are they "doable?" If they are, then the execution of the material plan will be done using a daily schedule going out to each work center on the factory floor and usually a weekly schedule going out to each vendor. The capacity plan will be executed by monitoring to see if actual output is meeting the plan.

Exec   Okay, so that's what people mean by "closing the loop." Putting in the other elements that are required to plan production and inventories in a manufacturing business. What's this MRP II we've been hearing about just recently?

OW   Once again, it was the users who took the tools they had and extended them. Manufacturing Resource Planning (MRP II) is a game plan for planning and monitoring all of the resources of a manufacturing company; manufacturing, marketing, finance, and engineering. Technically, it involves using the closed loop MRP system to generate the financial figures. Figure 2, for example, shows a regular material requirements planning format expressed in dollars. This is the pump component inventory plan derived from the material requirements plan. The first figure in the projected available balance row, 540,000, is the summary of the "on hand" inventory of components expressed in dollars taken from the material requirements plan. The requirements are also costed out, the scheduled receipts and planned orders (lumped together under "scheduled receipts" in the figure) are costed out, and a projected component inventory balance is calculated. This is the **right** level of stores inventory to have to support the current production rate for these pumps. If the master schedule is correct, it's a valid plan and actual performance can be monitored against it. A valid purchase commitment report (as opposed to the ones that are derived from order launching and expediting with a huge "bubble" of past due material) can be developed. Manufactured items can be broken out of the plan, and converted to capacity requirements in standard hours by work center. These can be costed out to show the amount of labor as well as the amount of material that needs to be purchased to meet a given plan. That was the first step in developing MRP II. Instead of having one set of numbers for the operating system in manufacturing and another set kept by the financial people, once the manufacturing people have numbers that are valid, the financial people can use these to get their numbers. Of course, whenever there are two systems, the numbers are bound to be different. With MRP II, everybody can be working to the same set of numbers.

Pump Component Inventory — in $(000)

		Month			
		1	2	3	4
Projected Gross Requirements		250	250	300	300
Scheduled Receipts		250	250	270	290
Proj. Avail. Bal.	540	540	540	510	500

Figure 2.   Pump Component

But that's only the **technical** difference. The big difference comes in the way management uses these tools now that the operating plans can be translated into the common denominator of business: dollars.

MRP II is literally a simulation of a manufacturing business. It can be used to schedule the factory, schedule vendors, plan manpower far better, plan capacity requirements for new equipment more accurately farther into the future and with more capability of testing various plans. It can be used to generate the planned shipping dollars, it can be tied in with the business plan, and it can be used to simulate "what ifs" like: "What if we have to get this product out on a rush basis in 30 days, what extra capacity will be needed, what other jobs might have to be pushed aside?", "What if marketing **really** sells what they are saying in that new product line, will we be able to support their sales projection with material and capacity?", "What if we introduce all those new products at once, how much additional inventory will we require?" In short, Manufacturing Resource Planning becomes a company game plan for manufacturing, marketing, engineering, and finance.

Exec   It sure sounds like MRP II can do some powerful things.

OW   You're right, but that's the wrong way to say it. MRP II is just a set of tools that enables management to run a manufacturing business far more professionally. The system itself is just a simple set of logical techniques that the massive data manipulation capability of the computer has made practical. What **people** have learned to do with it is its real power. In the past, for example, there was usually an adversary relationship between manufacturing, marketing, engineering, and finance. They didn't have a common game plan, and they typically didn't work together as a team as well as they should have. Now we can have that game plan. Now it's up to management to use the game plan and develop an environment where teamwork is the norm rather than the exception. Americans are very individualistic — "one man, one vote." Our toughest competitors, the Japanese, are great team players. They play well together even when there **isn't** a game plan. We need the game plan, we've got it now. It isn't "miracle requirements planning," but it is the missing link.

Exec   I guess one thing still bothers me. Why did you call it "Manufacturing Resource Planning"? Many people are still going to think of it as something that applies only to manufacturing.

OW   That was a toughie. We could have called it something new, but I think the world is getting tired of three letter words and acronyms. It's about time we settled things down and showed management that we have a standard set of tools on the operations side of the business, just as the financial people have standard costs, budgets, cash flow, etc. Manufacturing Resource Planning did develop out of material requirements planning and that's still the scheduling guts of the system. And scheduling is fundamental in running a manufacturing business. Fundamental not just to manufacturing, but fundamental to finance (cash flow is built around timing), fundamental to marketing (customer delivery performance is built around timing), fundamental to engineering (without schedules in engineering, new product introduction, engineering change, and the delivery of highly engineered products simply won't take place on time, and the rest of the planning in a manufacturing business won't work well). Some people prefer to call it things like "Management Resource Planning" or "Business Requirements Planning," but this is not planning that applies to a theatrical agency or a real estate business, it applies to a **manufacturing** business. Perhaps our biggest problem is that we often fail to recognize that our businesses are manufacturing businesses; not that manufacturing is more important than marketing, engineering, and finance, but that **all** of the resources in a manufacturing business must be planned and coordinated properly if we're to get the best results.

Exec   It sounds like this has dramatic potential. Why don't we hear more about it? Certainly, there are occasional articles, but you would think that all of the business publications would be doing everything possible to accelerate the adoption of MRP II.

OW   Any new technology takes 20 to 30 years to really sink in. The airplane was invented in 1903, commercial airlines became a success a long, long time later. We have a new industrial revolution going on today. An ability to run a manufacturing business far more professionally. An ability very much akin to the quantum leap in professionalism that came in flying with the development of instruments. Running a business with MRP II **is** like flying by instruments. It gives the managers far more capability than they ever had before. But when we are in the midst of a revolution, it's difficult to see what's happening, because we are too close to it. I'm sure not too many managers during the first industrial revolution said to their wives, "Skip breakfast this morning, honey. I don't want to be late for the industrial revolution." When the most dramatic things are taking place, we are usually too close to the day-to-day activity to recognize their significance. Nevertheless, we have some powerful tools available today, and if we are going to regain our position as the leader in manufacturing in the world, it behooves us to get these tools adopted and used effectively as quickly as possible.

Chapter 2

Does MRP II Apply to *My* Business?

Exec　We have a large corporation with many divisions. Are you implying that MRP will apply to **all** of these divisions? For example, we have one division making machine tools. They have a large backlog of customer orders that usually extends 18 months or more into the future. We don't make-to-forecast and it doesn't seem to me that the problems of change that MRP addresses are really part of that business.

OW　There is no question that when you have a firm backlog of customer orders, you have the best available "forecast." And it's interesting that people are always complaining about poor forecasts, yet in the typical company as their backlog of orders goes up, their **inventory** goes up too! That would seem to indicate that having a valid forecast isn't the solution to the problems of scheduling. Of course, in practice, most companies' order backlogs jiggle around like a bowl of jelly. But there are many other changes that have nothing to do with the forecast. Machines that break down, tooling that breaks, processes that go awry (there probably isn't a major manufacturing company in the country where there isn't some process — like chrome plating — that's a little marginal today, even though it worked well until last night on the four to twelve shift!). There are engineering changes, key people who are absent, vendor material that gets rejected, vendors that deliver late, and carriers who temporarily lose material. Manufacturing is a world of **change** and schedules, as a consequence, have to change or they won't reflect true need dates.

Exec　What about a company making a highly engineered product? Does it apply there?

OW　That's a very common question because people making a highly engineered product typically see MRP as a better way to order material, and ordering material isn't one of their biggest problems as long as they can get the documentation from engineering on time. But, consider a company making extruders. They had one order that was three months late because the drive unit hadn't been **designed** yet! The plant manager said, "If I got the prints and documentation tomorrow, it would be another three months before we could ship that order." Another order was one month past due for lack of an electric motor from Westinghouse; yet there was a Westinghouse motor sitting in the pile of parts that had been set aside for the job that was three months past due! The motors were very similar, although not identical. But if MRP had been used properly, Westinghouse would have been notified to reschedule the motor for the job held up for lack of the drive unit to a later need date, and they could have worked on the motor for the job that actually needed it. They actually worked on the **oldest** order first, and since the motor that wasn't needed showed an earlier due date (since it was three months past due, rather than one month past due) they sent the wrong motor to the customer — in good faith. The customer, by failing to reschedule properly, kept the job that was one month past due from being shipped. Even though a company makes a highly engineered product, their need for reschedules to keep up with the constant change is as bad as, or worse than, other kinds of manufacturing companies. And MRP II can also help with bidding, order promising, capacity planning, financial planning, and the "what if" questions.

Exec   But, frequently, engineering itself holds up manufacturing. They don't get the information to them on time.

OW   Material requirements planning is a network planning technique. It is similar to PERT (Project Evaluation and Review Technique), PMS (Project Management System), and CPM (Critical Path Method). They are all network scheduling techniques, but MRP is the simplest one. Some companies today use the same program they use for material requirements planning to plan activities for their engineering resources — the system doesn't know that a number represents an activity rather than a part! This way they have one common, simple system that they use for planning engineering as well as manufacturing. The downfall of sophisticated systems like PERT was that they were used once or twice for the original planning, but they were never kept up to date because they were not straightforward, simple, and understandable to the users.

Exec   What about our wire and cable plant? It's hard for me to visualize how MRP would apply there.

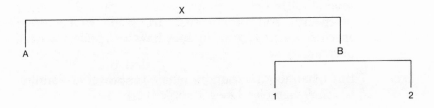

Figure 3.   The Assembled Product

OW   Figure 3 shows the bill of material schematic for a company making an assembled product. X is the assembly, A and B are subassemblies, and subassembly B is made up of parts 1 and 2. Wire and cable has an upside down bill of material, like that shown in Figure 4.

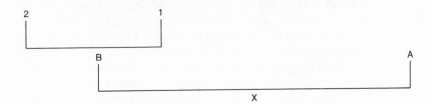

Figure 4.   The Upside Down Bill of Material

Rod is drawn into wire. The wire can be tinned, or not tinned. Then it can be stranded to different numbers of strands, and it can then be given types of extruded covering, at which point the wires go to a cabler which is an assembly operation with a "right-side-up" bill of material. The upside down bill of material applies in many situations. A steel mill, for example, takes ingots and makes them into billets, rolls them into sheets, slits them into strips, rolls them down to finished size, and once again has scheduling problems; but they are not the classical fabrication and assembly type problems even though they are just as complex. One company makes forged rings that are later made into gears, etc. One forging blank in rough form can be made into several different forgings that are carried in their inventory, and others that are made to customer specifications. Once again, they have an upside down bill of material.

Exec   But what about a foundry where the material planning is usually simple? Does it apply there?

OW   I've been addressing the application of material requirements planning in your previous questions. One of the reasons that there is a lot of confusion over the application of MRP is that we think of the material scheduling only. Think of the closed loop schematic shown in Figure 1 once again. Certainly, a foundry must have a sales & operations plan and a master schedule. Planning material requirements may well be very straightforward. In some foundries, it could be done with a pencil on the back of an envelope. (In others, cores are often a holdup, and the maintenance and repair of core boxes is a problem — cores could be scheduled with MRP very effectively.) But certainly a foundry needs to do capacity requirements planning; it has to have some kind of scheduling in the shop, and some kind of monitoring of capacity. The closed loop system applies to any kind of manufacturing business imaginable, even if the material requirements planning part of it isn't critical. And I would call it closed loop MRP even if the business was so simple that all of this planning — and **replanning** — could be done manually. If one were to sit down and invent a way to plan activities in a manufacturing business, there is no way to escape the closed loop logic.

Exec   We have one consumer products division where the manufacturing cost is very low. When the cost of labor — and even material — is a small percentage of the sales dollar, would MRP offer much payoff?

OW   Let's think in terms of MRP II, the company game plan. In the cosmetics business, for example, the coordination of **all** of the activities in the business is one of the toughest problems of all. If a major advertising campaign to promote a new fragrance takes place before the fragrance is available at the retailer, most of the advertising expenditure was a waste of money. Two or three weeks later, the lady who is a potential customer will have forgotten the name of the fragrance. And here we have a real education job to do because scheduling isn't considered to be a real important issue in a cosmetics company. But it is when manufacturing, marketing, design, advertising and procurement each work to informal, ill-coordinated plans. And that's what MRP II is all about: making valid plans so that all of the functions of a manufacturing business can work together more effectively.

Exec   What about distribution? Isn't that really more of a pure inventory management problem?

OW   Too many people think that distribution is a "different" situation when it really isn't. The traditional tools of "inventory management" and distribution were: order point, economic order quantity, and "allocation algorithms." These have been around since the late '50s, but their track record is rather poor. It would be hard to point to companies today that are saying that they have accomplished a great deal using this kind of system, even though practically every seminar or textbook on distribution inventory management mentions these techniques as the standard "tools of the trade."

Consider this example: Imagine three branch warehouses, or distribution centers (DCs) as they are usually called today, that carry the same item and at each DC the inventory is just barely above order point.

At the main plant warehouse, there is a back-up inventory, and it's just barely above order point. Obviously, when these three warehouses break order point almost simultaneously, there will need to be a rush replenishment order placed at the main plant. On the other hand, consider a situation where each of the DCs has just received a resupply, but the main plant is just below order point, and a replenishment order is created that probably won't be needed for some time to come. **The classical order point system didn't address timing.** Using MRP in distribution (we call it DRP— Distribution **Resource** Planning— because today it is being tied in with the financial, the traffic, the warehouse systems, and manufacturing planning), the forecast will be extended in time periods— typically weeks — into the future. Planned order releases will be created for each of the DCs and these will become the requirements against the main plant inventory. As demand changes, these requirements will change and messages indicating necessary reschedules will be generated. The DRP approach emphasizes timing, scheduling, and, in practice, it has proved to be a breakthrough in handling distribution inventories.

Some companies make their own distribution inventories and very few of them coordinate the distribution activities and the manufacturing activities well. By using the DRP approach, they will be far better off in terms of inventory investment, plant efficiency, and customer service. Other companies simply purchase and resell material. By using the DRP approach, they can show their suppliers their requirements much farther into the future, keep their requirements up to date so that they represent their real, current needs, and extend these requirements out beyond the vendors' lead times so that as vendors change lead times, they won't need to respond to these changes.

Exec   It sounds like we're talking about each of our divisions using the same system. That alone could be a great advantage to management if everybody was talking the same language.

OW   Yes, we have clients who feel very strongly about that. One I can think of has seven plants in the United States, and they all use the same kind of planning and monitoring system. Even their Mexican and overseas plants all talk the same "MRP language."

Exec   Okay, Ollie, I've got one needle for you. Back in the '60s, everybody talked about order point — you included. In the '70s and '80s, we're talking about MRP, what comes next?

OW   That's a good question! Another question that is similar to that is, "I've heard about the MRP system, what are the other choices?" The answer to both questions is the same. We finally learned how to develop a formal system that simulates the fundamental manufacturing equation that was always used in the informal system: "What are we going to make, what does it take to make it, what have we got, what have we got to get." Any system that simulates that equation is, by definition, MRP. Any system that **doesn't** will be supplemented by an informal system that **does** simulate that equation. What are the alternatives? **To use MRP or have the shortage list be the real schedule.** What comes after MRP? Well, we can call it what we will in the future, but unless we somehow figure out a way to change the fundamental manufacturing equation, it's going to look an awful lot like MRP!

Chapter 3

What Results Can We Expect?

Exec   I've heard of some rather dramatic results in companies that are using MRP well. Where do I look for these results?

OW   The results translate into one basic word — PRODUCTIVITY. Let me first summarize the kinds of results people get and then we'll talk about each of these in more detail:

1. Reduced inventory.
2. Improved customer service.
3. Improved direct labor productivity.
4. Reduced purchased costs.
5. Reduced traffic costs.
6. Reduced obsolescence.
7. Reduced overtime.
8. Having the numbers to run the business.
9. Having accountability throughout the organization.
10. Improved quality of life.

Exec   Well, I've read plenty on productivity today — you have to be hiding in a cave to miss all of the literature that addresses that subject — but I rarely read anything about MRP II and productivity. Why is that if MRP II is so good?

OW   I read the articles on productivity myself, and I truly question how many of them were ever written by anybody who knows much about what really goes on in a manufacturing business. Virtually everybody assumes that manufacturing businesses run the way they should run, and that simply isn't true. They assume that the formal scheduling system works, **and nothing could be farther from the truth!** Unfortunately, there's a lot of flailing around in addressing the productivity problem. Most of the discussions come from people who don't understand the problem and, consequently, don't understand the solution.

Exec   Well, let's talk about inventory reduction. With the cost of money today and the fact that money is often difficult to borrow at any price, that's becoming very critical in our company.

OW   Making more of the right things at the right time can result in an inventory reduction. The typical MRP user — and I mean one that is doing it reasonably well, not one that has just generated paper from a computer — will get a 1/4 to 1/3 reduction in inventory investment. This translates directly into the productivity of money. When this money can be freed up, it can be used to invest in more efficient machinery, and other tools to improve productivity.

Exec   I know how to reduce inventory — if I insist on a reduction, **it will happen!** I'm really kidding, Ollie, because I know, as well as you, that inventory reduction by edict will soon show up in poor customer service. Some of my people say that when we reduce inventory we dip into our safety stock, so we're bound to hurt customer service.

OW   That was the old thinking in the order point inventory model: "Lead time is fixed and known, and the more safety stock the better the customer service." A "model" isn't a model if it doesn't represent the real world — and in the real world, lead time is highly variable — depending a great deal on how much we expedite. In the real world, no one tried to get something into stock on the due date if they knew there was a safety stock— and the more safety stock, the less they believed the schedules. **MRP emphasizes scheduling** — and better scheduling can result in reduced inventory **and** improved service.

I can't think of any good MRP user that hasn't improved customer service dramatically. One company making laboratory instruments went from 52 percent to 90 percent on time delivery, and they believe they can hit over 95 percent very soon. Think what this means in terms of the productivity of the marketing efforts! Think what it means in terms of the productivity of sales people who can go out and get new orders rather than spend their time apologizing for the fact that the last order wasn't shipped on time. Consider service parts, a real concern for the customer who is concerned with the productivity of **his** equipment. Many companies that don't schedule well put other companies into the business of supplying parts for their products — and then call them "pirates"! The tragedy of this is that service parts usually have a very high markup. Handled well, service parts can make a disproportionate contribution to the profit picture.

Exec   You keep talking about productivity — does MRP II really have all that much impact on the productivity of direct labor?

OW   You bet. Of course, it varies substantially from company to company. The highest potential comes from the assembly area because that's the one that suffers the most from part shortages. Twenty to 40 percent improvement in productivity in assembly is not at all unusual. In the supplying operations, 5 to 10 percent improvement in productivity is about average because there is less expediting, fewer break-ins to setups, more of the right material available at the right time, etc. After an MRP system has been on the air for a while, there are even greater improvements in productivity. The bulk of the typical foreman's time today is spent expediting material, looking for material, in shortage meetings, getting product out the door with a big "push" at the end of the month, recovering from the end-of-the-month "push," moving people around on short notice to cover problems that have occurred, etc. Most companies estimate that between 60 and 80 percent of the average foreman's time is spent trying to get the job done in spite of poor schedules. The foreman's job description says, "Manage your people, direct your people, educate your people, install better methods, make sure the tooling is right, make sure the quality is right." MRP II users have proven that when foremen have time to do their jobs, productivity can improve substantially.

Exec   What about purchased costs? That seems to be a tough one because we have so little real control over our vendors.

OW   Just because purchased cost is "on the other side of the wall" doesn't mean it's beyond control. Read the magazines and articles on purchasing. They talk about value analysis, better negotiation, better sourcing to reduce cost, working with engineering to standardize product and reduce cost, having yearly contracts, "blanket orders and releases" with vendors; but purchasing people don't have time to do all of these things well. And whenever they set up release rates with the vendors, the release rates are rapidly out of synchronization with actual production requirements. Purchasing people spend 60 to 80 percent of their time on expediting and paperwork such as purchase orders, requisitions, and reschedules. With an MRP system, the purchase order as such does not exist. There is a yearly letter of agreement, and a weekly computer-generated schedule that goes to the vendor. Since there are no purchase orders for material used in production, no requisitions, and no reschedules (these are built right into the vendor's schedule) far less time is spent on paperwork. Since need dates are valid in a well managed MRP system, far less time is spent on expediting. This gives purchasing people more time to do the things that can reduce purchased costs.

Exec   What kind of reduction in purchased costs should the typical company look for?

OW   The national average runs about 5 percent, and that's a lot of money when you figure that most manufacturing companies spend about three dollars on purchased material for every dollar they spend on direct labor. A 5 percent reduction in purchased costs is like a 15 percent improvement in the productivity of direct labor. One company with MRP, for example, held their material cost increases to 2 percent in a year when inflation went up 11 percent. But this is highly dependent on the kind of business. A cigarette manufacturer using huge volumes of tobacco and paper,

for example, is not likely to be able to reduce purchased costs through better scheduling. On the other
hand, a manufacturer of machine tools that purchases
a great deal of raw material components and subassemblies has an excellent opportunity to do this.

Exec   Purchasing claims that much of our air freight would
be unnecessary with better scheduling.

OW   The American automobile industry in 1979 spent over
100 million dollars on premium air freight. That figure
probably doesn't include the amount of money their
vendors spent on premium air freight, nor does it
include the cost of their own airplanes. Much of
this additional traffic cost was due to poor scheduling.
They can't afford to have line shortages, but their
scheduling isn't that good in the short term. And any
time we add cost to a product without increasing value,
we are reducing productivity. Other companies spend
a great deal of money on premium air freight **delivering**
their product to their customers because their scheduling isn't good. Once again, this has a direct impact on
productivity because this cost will have to be passed on
to the customer sooner or later.

Exec   We have some hi-tech divisions where obsolescence,
your next topic, really is hurting. But it seems to me
that obsolescence "comes with the territory" in this
type of business.

OW   **Change** "comes with the territory" — and that's what
MRP is geared to. The biggest single cause of
obsolescence is uncontrolled engineering change. And
without good scheduling, the planning and coordination of engineering change is not going to take place as
effectively as it should. Many engineering changes
require using up existing supplies of components.
Sometimes these components have to be used up in
matched sets, and the timing of the engineering change
must be planned and monitored closely because things
will change in the manufacturing environment. Other
companies make products like pharmaceuticals that
have a shelf life. Once again, MRP, with its emphasis

on timing, can be used to reduce — notice I didn't say "eliminate" — obsolescence in this kind of industry.

Exec   It isn't too hard to imagine how MRP can help to reduce overtime; and that is not only expensive. We are also finding that our workers don't like to work overtime like they used to. They want the time off.

OW   In addition to the informal scheduling system we talked about, there also was an informal capacity planning system. MRP replaces the informal system — the shortage list — with a formal scheduling system. In the same way, the informal capacity planning system that responded to problems after they happened, for the most part, can be replaced with a system that simulates what will happen in the future. Because of this enhanced planning capability, it's not unusual to see companies that have reduced their overtime to one tenth of what it was before they had MRP. This translates directly into more productivity per labor dollar. But there is more to the overtime problem than most people recognize. Anyone who has run a manufacturing company soon realizes that chronic overtime is very nonproductive. When people work more than three or four Saturdays in a row in a manufacturing company, their output starts to fall off due to fatigue and the fact that they start taking other days off the following week to make up for the leisure time they have missed. This means that the company is paying for six days of work (not to mention the overtime premium) while getting only five days' work. One manufacturing company that used to work three shifts seven days a week was able, through the better planning of materials and capacity, to get more output working three shifts five days per week after they installed MRP.

Exec   I'm particularly interested in the comments you made earlier about "getting the numbers to run the business." I find it difficult, however, to make a connection between better scheduling and our financial controls.

OW   Well, consider the "purchased commitment" report. It is made up by costing out the open purchased orders and adding them up by time periods. Because order launching and expediting generated a large "phoney backlog," there was always a big bubble of past due material. But all of the material past due and due in the first month never did show up in any one month. If that amount of material ever did come in, the company would have been in great financial trouble, and they probably wouldn't have had room to store the material! Because the operating system didn't work, the financial numbers didn't work; then the financial people had to develop fudge factors and, in fact, had no plan to compare against to determine whether the amount of material on order was correct even if they **did** believe it. Once we have an MRP II system operating, the financial figures are derived from the operating figures. In a manufacturing business, until the numbers work well in manufacturing, it's going to be difficult to make them work well many other places. But once they do, the accounting system can get its numbers from the manufacturing numbers. A great many companies today, for example, cycle count their inventory. This is a sampling technique, a quality control type technique, for measuring performance. This cycle counting is usually done on a daily basis. If inventory records are accurate, they can be certified by an auditing firm; and there will be no need for the annual physical inventory— one of the **least productive** efforts that most manufacturing companies get involved in. Once again, if the manufacturing numbers are right, they can be used to generate the accounting numbers.

Exec   Another comment you made that intrigues me is this comment about accountability. My experience is that true accountability throughout the organization is easy to talk about, but tough to make stick in the real world.

OW   In a typical manufacturing company, accountability only exists at the top. Since accountability implies measurement, measurement requires a valid plan. We can measure the general manager on whether or not we hit the shipping budget, but we sure can't measure the assembly foreman on whether he did his job when he didn't have the parts. We can't measure the machine shop foreman on whether he did his job when his schedule wasn't valid. We can't measure the purchasing people on whether they did their job when their schedule wasn't valid. And we can't measure the scheduling people on whether they did their job properly when, in most companies, management didn't even provide them with the tools to make valid schedules! With MRP II, we **can** make valid plans, we **can** measure performance. And accountability to meet a plan **can** exist throughout the organization.

Exec   Quality of life is something we're all talking about today. Job enrichment. But isn't the hassle kind of "built in" to a manufacturing business — especially if you demand high performance?

OW   Once people can start working together to a game plan they all understand, there's a lot less adversary relationship, a great deal more satisfaction when the product is going out the door, and people can see the results of the efforts that they are making. Imagine how a foreman who has just hit his schedule 100 percent — and that's not unusual with MRP — feels when he goes home at night. Imagine how a manufacturing vice president who has just hit his quarterly objectives, and is also being complimented by the marketing people, feels when he goes home at night. Imagine how anyone in a company that is able to see the results of their efforts feels, especially when most of their experience has been with the frustration of the informal system. As one manufacturing vice president said, "It certainly is a treat to be right instead of always being wrong!"

Exec   The results you talk about are so good that they're hardly credible. Are you talking potential or reality?

OW   Reality. Every bit of it can be documented. And if you really understand the problems in manufacturing and think about it, it isn't too surprising. With the informal system, we simply couldn't schedule properly. Not just in the factory, we couldn't coordinate our activities in the entire organization. Scheduling is fundamental to the effective operation of a manufacturing enterprise; and that's what MRP II is all about. It's fascinating how we love to get involved in the exotic and the esoteric, yet time and again, when we get right down to the real problems, they revolve around doing the fundamentals exceedingly well. And manufacturing companies are no exception to **that** rule.

Chapter 4

What Does MRP II Cost?

Exec   Well, the benefits of MRP sound great, but what about the costs?

OW   The costs fall into three basic categories: **Technical, Data,** and **People.** Let's break these out.

In the **TECHNICAL** area we have:

1. **The cost of hardware.** Most companies today have a computer. Installing an MRP system may require some additional costs for more capacity, typically file capacity, like extra disc drives or terminals.

2. **The cost of software.** These are the computer programs for doing MRP. That would include the capacity planning, dispatching, financial reporting, etc. required for MRP II.

3. **The cost of systems and data processing people assigned to the project.**

In the **DATA** area we have:

1. **The master schedule.**
2. **Work centers.**
3. **Cost figures.**

These typically don't involve a lot of preparation for MRP.

4. **Bills of material.**
5. **Inventories.**
6. **Routings.**

These do and they can be quite costly. They will be discussed below.

In the **PEOPLE** area we have:

1. **Education,** both at live classes and using video courses.
2. **Professional guidance from a qualified consultant.**

Exec   How do you estimate the hardware costs?

OW   If you don't have a computer, you've got to get some computer resources that can handle the number of components and the number of levels in the bill of material that you have for your product. Some companies can operate with a computer that costs as little as $50,000 a year to lease; others spend as much as $50,000 per month. It's largely a function of the number of components, the complexity of the bill of material, the length of the planning horizon, etc. And you don't really need to own your own hardware. It can be done by teleprocessing, using a corporate computer or using a service bureau computer; or it can be done by a service bureau in a batch processing mode. Today, the costs of the hardware are down very dramatically and they will continue to improve in price/performance in the future. It's important to recognize in the hardware area that there are some one-time costs, especially if the hardware is being purchased; and some recurring costs that would occur if the hardware was being leased.

Exec   What about the cost of the software?

OW   Here again, prices vary all over the lot from about $15,000 a year for software from the computer suppliers themselves, to a $300,000 one-time price and $30,000 a year to maintain a sophisticated system from a software house. Often some of the more expensive software will require less work to make it usable. In many cases, however, the additional cost is just for "features" that frequently turn out to be bells and whistles that don't have any great, practical value. It's important to select software carefully and, in our reference section at the back of the book, we tell you more about how to do that. Practically every software package you can get will need some modification to make it usable, not because it needs to be tailored to your business so much as the fact that it needs to be made into usable MRP. That's indicative of the adolescence of the software field today, especially where manufacturing applications are concerned.

Exec   What about the cost of systems and programming people? How many are likely to be required?

Obviously, here we're going to have a one-time as well as a recurring cost as you discussed above.

OW It's very difficult to pin this figure down because it can range from one or two systems and programming people in a small company where there aren't many programs to interface with, to much greater numbers in a corporate environment where many interfaces are required. Many companies are able to install an MRP system with three or four computer systems and programming people. It's important to avoid overwhelming the project with people. One large corporation has one hundred people working on their MRP project — mostly systems and programming people. I give them little hope for ever achieving anything because they are so overstaffed that they are bound to become a debating "committee," not at all action-oriented. We had an Executive Conference where we invited six chief executives from six successful MRP users to tell us about the results they got and what they would have done over. One of the questions from the audience was, "How many extra people did you actually add?" Only one company added extra people — **two people** — and they were both in the stores area. They had no real out-of-pocket costs for systems and programming people because they simply used the ones they had and applied them to the MRP project. Some companies even then would **allocate** the cost to the project and that's certainly their prerogative.

Exec I'm surprised at the small numbers of people you're talking about. I hear you recommending that we run lean and hard. I've heard corporations talk about twenty to thirty people assigned to the project, but you say that's not the right way to go?

OW I doubt that you have heard those kinds of numbers from the successes.

Exec What about fixing bills of material?

OW This includes correcting them and restructuring them to make sure they represent the way the products must be planned and scheduled in many cases. Our experience says that this may take in the range of two to six man years (two men one year, three men two years, etc.). We have seen companies that had to allocate even more people to the job.

Exec   What about the cost of correcting routings?

OW   That generally turns out to be somewhat less than the cost of correcting bills of material. It might be one to four man years. Remember, of course, I'm quoting average kinds of figures that could be very different from one company to another. I just want to give you some kind of a bench mark. I know companies where bills of material and routings were both so good that they had practically no work to do to get them corrected in preparing for MRP. Those companies are the **exception,** however.

Exec   What about the cost of correcting inventory records? I'm not sure I'm clear where these costs actually are incurred.

OW   I'm not surprised because it isn't something as simple as taking an extra "physical inventory" to correct the records. Companies typically have taken physicals at least once a year in the past, and none of them eliminated the problems so there's no reason to believe that another physical will! The real problem is in assigning accountability for transaction integrity, and that requires limited access stores. No person will accept the responsibility for making sure transactions take place as material moves without limited access stores. This doesn't necessarily mean "locked stockrooms." It does mean that there is someone at the door of the stockroom so that only authorized people can go in and out. It does mean that if material is stored in the yard area because it's extremely bulky, the yard becomes a limited access storage area even though it doesn't have a roof. The real cost of inventory record integrity comes in factories that weren't designed to have good physical control of material. The typical airplane manufacturer, automobile manufacturer, truck manufacturer, etc. usually has an assembly line sneaking down through the middle of an enormous wall-to-wall stockroom; and they have all of the short term scheduling problems that go with lack of inventory record integrity. Some companies have had to spend as much as $400,000 to re-layout their plant to give them control over stores. One school bus company that did this has found that it was an excellent investment because now they can get the right material to the right place at the right time because they have the numbers they can use to run an effective MRP system. If the numbers aren't right, MRP can only multiply them and extend them into more wrong numbers. It never corrects them. Accurate inventories weren't particularly significant in the days of the shortage list. With MRP, they are essential.

Exec   What about the cost of education and how do we do that?

OW   Live education classes are one of the indispensable ways to educate some key people. This will usually range from 5 to 10 percent of the total population of the company. In a small company with a couple of hundred people, it would probably be wise to send 20 people to live classes. In a company with 2,000 people, 100 people might be adequate. The percentage is lower in the larger company, based on the experience of our clients.

Exec   But I've heard that we have to educate practically everyone in the company. Certainly that can't all be done through live classes.

OW   That's right. The way to get to the rest of the group is through video courses. The people who have attended the live classes should now be accountable for educating their people using the video courses. That doesn't mean that they have to spend a lot of time in each video class. It does mean that they need to make sure that their people are there and that they attend, at least, the discussion sessions to be sure that their people understand what they are learning. These people, in turn, have to educate **their** people. It is a kind of a chain letter approach with line accountability for education — and I emphasize that. The personnel department, for example, can be a great help; but they cannot be held **accountable** — line management must be.

Exec   What about continuing education?

OW   Video courses should continue to be used. Some key people should be sent back to live classes after several years. And there is also an executive conference available for people to use as a means of getting an update.

Exec   Ollie, I'm sure you can take another needle! I do notice that when it comes to selecting software, one of your companies provides a service to help us do that. When it comes to live education, you have two companies that will do that. When we need video courses, we can go to another one of your companies for that. And you also supply the books that we will require. It certainly seems like an interesting coincidence!

OW   Your jibe is a good one. But it certainly is no coincidence. In 1968, after 13 years in manufacturing, and 3 years experience in educating executives on manufacturing applications at IBM where I was Manager of Industry Education for Manufacturing, I decided to leave to get into professional education. My associates told me that I was crazy to leave IBM! The consultants that I knew said that no consultant had ever really made money at education. But I felt that this was what was **needed** from my observations of the few successes and the many frustrating failures of the computer that I had seen in manufacturing companies. When I started making video courses in 1971, once again it was with a great deal of trepidation. Everybody said, "You're cutting your own throat. Who will come to your live classes?", but I felt that massive education was badly needed, and that this was the only solution no matter what the consequences. (Luckily, they turned out well!) To make a long story short, each of our activities was started to address a particular problem like education, software selection, etc. The only reason we publish our own books is that it cuts the lead time from manuscript to publication by about 12 months. I never wanted to be in the book publishing business and I'm still not crazy about it. But our business is helping people to be successful with MRP II — and we'll do just about anything required to accomplish that.

Exec   What about in-plant education done by an outside consultant? I've noticed that you don't have a company to do that.

OW   You're right, and that's called "putting your money where your mouth is!" I don't believe that that's an effective method. It isn't as good as live classes because it doesn't get people outside of their company where they can really open their minds. It tends to reinforce the "we're unique, we're different" approach. It lacks the peer confirmation of being with people from other companies. And it tends to be a one-shot deal. It isn't as good as video either. Certainly, one of your general foremen — who's attended a live class and is teaching his people using video — is going to have a lot more credibility with his people than some outside consultant. I've not seen the approach where the outside expert comes in for a few days to give everybody "smart pills" really work. That's why we don't use it.

Exec   What should we think about, then, for costs of education?

OW   For live classes, once you've figured out how many people you want to attend, you should estimate about $2,500 per person, including tuition, hotel expense, meals, travel expense, etc. Remember, when you're counting the number of people coming to class, one individual may get counted twice. One person might go to one of the live MRP classes and also go to one of the bill of material classes described in the reference section. The video library typically leases for between 20 and 30 thousand dollars a year, depending primarily on the number of people to be educated. With the video libraries we supply, there is a tailored education program made by a professional education consultant spelling out who should attend what courses, the content of the courses for each group of people in your company, what tapes should be used in each session, etc. There is more information on the video courses in the reference section.

Exec   What about professional guidance. Do you supply a consulting service?

OW   Virtually every company will need some outside consulting help to implement MRP II successfully from what we've observed. A good consultant will, in my opinion, be the "catalyst," coming in about one day every 4 to 6 weeks for the duration of the project. Plan on about 15 visits at a cost for travel, fees, etc. of approximately $2,000 per visit. To answer your question, we don't have much capacity to do consulting ourselves, but we have associates — who run their own consulting businesses — who could supply this service. People we can endorse.

Exec   Okay, we've talked about payout and we've talked about costs, and it's obvious that we'd have to get most of these numbers together for ourselves. What do you typically see in terms of payout from an MRP project in total dollars?

OW   In every one of our live classes, as well as working with clients, I do a sample justification using an actual company in the room, and using numbers supplied by people from that company. The worst justification I can recall gave an 80 percent annual return on the cost of installing MRP. In other words, if the cost was $600,000, the annual return was $480,000. And that's a recurring return. Once money is taken out of inventory, the inventory interest cost (we don't use inventory "carrying cost," just interest cost in the justification) will come back every year as long as the inventory is operated at a lower level. The best justification I can remember at the moment was a 1200 percent annual return. In other words, if the system was going to cost approximately $600,000 to install, the annual return was $7,200,000 per year recurring. The average payback runs about three to one.

There is, of course, cash flow to be kept in mind. The typical MRP system takes about 18 months to install, and it's all negative cash flow during that period. The kind of return that we're talking about should come back within the first full year that MRP II is on the air if it is installed and managed properly.

Chapter 5

Why Should the *Executive* Care?

Exec   I hear much ado about top management "support" and "involvement" if MRP is going to succeed. I'm not sure I understand why this is so necessary.

OW   I don't think either of those words really conveys the point. "Support" without understanding is a liability. And management surely doesn't need to spend a lot of time and get terribly "involved" in the nitty gritty of MRP like determining lot sizing rules. What's required is management leadership to install and operate it properly.

Exec   I still don't see why the executive has to be so involved — sorry — "provide leadership" to make a scheduling system work.

OW   But MRP II, Manufacturing Resource Planning, is **not** just a better scheduling system. A formal scheduling system that really works becomes the cornerstone of a real company game plan. It's a set of tools to run a business more professionally.

But to make it happen, there must be **a new set of values,** a new set of objectives. Inventory records have to be correct. The CEO will have to establish line accountability for meeting this objective. The bill of material can no longer just be a document that's of value to engineering and only used for reference by other parts of the company. It now becomes a control document. The master schedule can no longer be a "wish list." It has to be realistic. Top management, in some companies that have an MRP system, still believes in overstating the master schedule. This gives the same kind of results that order launching and expediting did. Many items are past due that aren't really needed. It doesn't take people very long to figure out that the system isn't telling them what they really need and they quietly revert to the shortage list.

Exec   That's an interesting thought. We really didn't tell the truth in the past, did we?

OW   No, we typically used the master schedule, for example, as "motivational information" rather than operational information. Production control put dates on purchase orders that were early because they didn't believe that purchasing would deliver on time. Purchasing didn't try to meet the dates because they knew that the dates were wrong. MRP is a system that can enable us to deal with facts to tell the truth. But that's not what our experience has been in manufacturing. And top management has got to set the example.

Exec   Okay, I understand all that, and I'm ready to do that. But I hear you saying that I've got to do even more. Like what?

OW   Well, consider implementation. In a company where head count has to be reduced due to a drop off in business, if top management doesn't understand what the MRP project is, you can be sure that the people who will be layed off will be the people fixing the bills of material, doing the cycle counting, etc. The only companies I've ever seen that lived through a head count reduction and still kept their MRP implementation project going were those where top management **really understood** how essential these tools are to enable them to manage the business more professionally.

Exec   Alright, what about after implementation? Where does top management come in then?

OW   I gave a talk to five hundred people recently. Approximately three hundred of them were MRP users. I asked, "How many of you have a master scheduling policy that specifies that marketing and manufacturing must get together to review the master schedule at least monthly, and then it must be signed off on by the CEO?" Less than ten people raised their hands! Isn't that incredible? The master schedule is made so that manufacturing can produce what the customers need. Yet, the people who are representing the customers often look upon MRP as just some production control system that doesn't involve them because management never explained it properly to them. At that same meeting I asked, "How many of you have a production plan that is made monthly at a meeting with marketing, manufacturing, finance, and engineering, presided over by the CEO?" Approximately six people raised their hands! Here we have the most powerful tools ever available for taking management policy and plans and translating them into detailed plans for the entire organization. Yet, in the typical company using this kind of system, **management doesn't formally make the plans or make the policy!**

Exec   It's funny, isn't it, how we looked at MRP II as some kind of a computer system. It really is a set of tools that gives us some powerful controls on the business, isn't it?

OW   Yes. And another reason why management needs to understand is that they must set the example in using the system to manage. When it's time for inventory reduction, the top manager who doesn't understand MRP will start to sign all the requisitions for over five hundred dollars. The requisitions he cancels will come back to him regularly because until such time as the master schedule is changed, the computer will continue to generate them. The real handle on inventory reduction is the master schedule. The professional top executive won't ask to sign the requisitions, but instead will call in the master scheduler, marketing, and manufacturing to see what can be taken out of the master schedule to reduce inventory. When a hot order comes in, the top executive who doesn't understand the new tools will, undoubtedly, have it hand carried through the factory and "let the chips fall where they may." The top manager who understands the tools will give it to the master scheduler and say: "Get this hand carried through the factory, but tell me and tell marketing what's going to suffer in order to get this out." The top manager who understands what the MRP tools are will use them to help in preparing the capital budget, in planning inventory levels, and cash flow. The top manager who doesn't will continue to use a separate set of numbers, and then wonder why what actually happens never coincides with the business plans.

Exec When you say top management, how far up are you going? Should we try to talk to the chairman of the board and even the board of directors?

OW Yes. I've seen companies where they went to a lot of trouble and expense to install MRP. Then the board of directors and the chairman hired a new president for a division — one with no real MRP II experience — who destroyed it all overnight. The minute there was a problem, he insisted on looking at the shortage lists and rolling up his sleeves and chasing shortages. Believe me. I didn't make that example up; I've seen it. It's tragic.

Exec Getting into MRP makes me feel almost like I'm getting married.

OW Not a bad comparison. Once you've operated with MRP your life will never be the same. We talked about the paybacks from MRP and talked about specifics. When I asked them at Xerox what they really felt they got from MRP that was of the greatest value, they said: "control" — the ability to control their dynamic, growing business. Manufacturing Resource Planning is a way to run a manufacturing business at a higher level of professionalism than we ever could before. The responsibility for running the business more professionally rests with management; and if they don't understand the new tools, they can't be expected to use them most effectively, or to set the example for other people in using the tools and placing a high priority on keeping the numbers correct.

Top management understanding is so critical that I tell companies that send people to other classes that they should really consider aborting MRP implementation until top management gets educated.

Chapter 6

What Must Be Done to Be Successful with MRP II?

Exec   I keep hearing that there has been a low success rate with MRP. Many have tried it, but only a small percentage have really succeeded.

OW   The truth of the matter is that so far a fairly small number — probably under 200 — have managed to become Class A or B MRP users. Class A companies use MRP II as a company game plan and can get along without a shortage list because they schedule so well. The B companies have a good closed loop MRP system — good "manufacturing control" — but don't really use it as a company game plan yet. The C companies use it primarily as an inventory control system. And the D companies have it working only in data processing. Even the C companies usually get an inventory reduction. The average inventory reduction from using MRP comes out to about one-third, according to a survey quoted in Business Week, June 4, 1979. This survey taken by Professors John Anderson and Roger Schroeder at the University of Minnesota included 326 companies. At that time, there weren't many Class A and B users in the United States, so it had to include many Class C users. Average delivery performance improved from 64 percent to 81 percent, and there were many other improvements from MRP. The real issue is that most MRP users **fall far short of its potential,** not that they fail. The miracle is that there aren't more **disasters** from MRP considering the way that the typical company blunders into it. To a great extent, success has been the biggest enemy of MRP. People hear what can be done using these tools and they rush headlong into it without the faintest notion of what they're doing.

Exec   What are the mistakes people make?

OW   They often pick a data processing person as the project leader. That ignores the issue of accountability; only a user can be accountable for making the tools produce results. They get very concerned about the software. This is like a golfer who has never played spending the first six months picking golf clubs, rather than learning about the game. Most software today is quite usable, and it isn't the software that makes the difference between success and failure in most installations. (Unless the software is so bad that it simply doesn't work — and that doesn't happen often today, thank goodness.) Because people think of MRP as a computer system, they make it sophisticated. They try to put the bells and whistles into the system hoping that this will make things work better, rather than recognizing that the system should be simple so that people understand what it means and can use the information confidently and effectively.

The way management approves of expenditures is a dead giveaway to their priorities. They've already got the computer in most companies, and they're spending a lot of money on it. They sign off on the expenditure for more software. They know that things that involve the computer cost a lot of money. When it comes to signing off on an appropriation for re-layout of the plant in order to have good physical control of stores, management is considerably less enthusiastic. When it comes to spending money for **education,** they tend to think of that as one of those nice luxuries we do every once in a while to kind of boost the morale of the people, rather than recognizing that it is a prerequisite to intelligent use of the better tools. Their priorities are **exactly backwards!** They should give education the highest priority on the plan, data integrity next, and software lowest. Not that they don't have to have software to do MRP. It must use standard MRP logic and it must work. But some of the best MRP installations in the country today use some of the most rudimentary software programs available.

Exec   I was interested in your comment about **people** having to make things work. We sure lost sight of that in the early days of the computer.

OW   Unfortunately, not everybody has learned from the school of hard knocks, but the people who are doing it successfully today learned the lessons and learned them well. The amateurs are waiting for the tools to actually do the job. But no computer ever added capacity, for example. Capacity is added by people who know what the numbers generated by the computer mean. These people, not the computer, will decide whether to work overtime, add manpower, buy more machinery, subcontract, use alternate routings, etc.

Exec   But why is it so different? What makes it so easy to take the wrong turn so frequently in developing an MRP system? From what I've heard, most people, given a choice, will make the wrong decision.

OW   There are really two basic reasons:

1. They perceive MRP to be a computer system rather than a people system made possible by the computer.

2. They fail to recognize that the major challenge will be for a lot of people to make the transition from the informal system environment to a formal system.

Running a manufacturing business with a formal system that works is simply not an extension of our experience. In the past, overstated master schedules were used regularly to "motivate the troops." Inventory record accuracy, for example, was not particularly important in the world of the shortage list. Even today, I hear of controllers who "don't believe in cycle counting." That's like a pilot who "doesn't believe in altimeters" — how else can inventory record accuracy be measured continuously? Today there is a body of knowledge. There is a set of standard tools available to the professional. But we've got a lot to do to get everybody to understand.

Exec   Can you summarize for me then, Ollie, **what** must be done to make MRP work?

OW   Yes. It all boils down to approaching this as a people system:

1. In the **technical** area, use a standard system. Don't fall for the old line "we're unique, we're different." The fundamental manufacturing equation applies to every manufacturing business I've ever seen, and I've been in over 1300 factories in the last 30 years and talked with thousands of executives. That doesn't necessarily mean that you have to use a purchased software program. You can write your own, but you must use standard logic. And don't let your people get the "computer virus" and complicate things. If people don't understand the logic of a system, they will not know why it told them to do what it did. Their choices are to obey it blindly or ignore it completely. Simplicity is a prerequisite to understanding. Understanding is a prerequisite to accountability. We have to teach people that the ultimate sophistication is simplicity.

2. In the **data** area, the most critical items are the bills of material, routings, and inventory records. (Work center identification, cost figures, and the master schedule are not usually areas that require major **development** efforts.) Inventory record accuracy will require:

   a. Setting that as an objective.

   b. Establishing line accountability from the top right down to the stores manager for inventory record accuracy.

   c. Measuring performance — using cycle counting, a daily sampling of the inventory records.

   d. Correcting the problems.

3. The **people** area mainly revolves around education.

   Everybody in the company should have some degree of education before MRP really goes on the air. Before the pilot goes on the air, 70 to 80 percent of the total population of the company should have some degree of education. Machine operators at the most successful companies get an hour of education each month, usually using about a half hour of video tape and a half hour of discussion with their foreman and perhaps some other member of management.

While everybody needs to be educated, two groups require particular attention: top management and first-line supervision like foremen. We talked about top management's role, and many people understand that today. But many people fail to recognize that real control will come from execution. And the execution of better schedules has to take place through the line organization. The foremen are the people who have to make it happen. They've usually heard about computer systems before, and they've usually seen few that produced anything but more paper, more work, and more frustration. MRP is simple. It's a way to predict the shortages farther into the future so that the foremen can be working **this** month to prevent next month's problems, rather than finding out about them one week before they happen. But if they don't understand MRP, and if they don't put as much effort into preventing problems as they do today into fixing problems after they happen, MRP will never attain its real potential.

Lastly, I would emphasize that education itself is not a fact transfer. That's why we don't recommend bringing in the outside expert to do the job. That's why there are so few educators who really have a track record of successful clients. There's never been a successful MRP installation without some torch-bearers. If the educators can't convey an enthusiasm for running the business more professionally, MRP simply won't happen. How, for example, does a company manage to operate, get shipments out the door, and tackle a project as ambitious as MRP? Obviously, they can't—and I told you earlier that they **don't**—add a lot of extra people. Temporary help isn't going to be very useful in fixing bills of material, for example. This has to be done with their own people. It means a lot of hard work from dedicated, enthusiastic people. And if education doesn't convey that enthusiasm, it is worthless.

Exec   What's the best environment for installing MRP? Is it a function of a company's size, its product, the complexity of its business, or what?

OW   Today, MRP can be applied economically in companies doing 2 million or more in sales because of the low cost of some of the computer hardware and software that is available. Frankly, it's easier to install MRP in a small company because there are fewer people to educate, fewer people who have to change the way they live. But large companies, like Xerox, have done it. It required a massive education program. The biggest problem with some large companies is that they tend to be very inbred and don't look outside to see what's going on because they "know" that they are doing it the best possible way. The automobile companies, for example, tend to suffer from a great deal of "intellectual incest" because they believe they are unique and different when, in fact, they aren't.

As for the product, that has practically nothing to do with it. The more complex the product, the more complex the scheduling problems, the more necessary it is to have MRP; but that doesn't mean that it's going to be a good environment for installing it. The environment really boils down to people and management. I look for a company where they have stability in the management. I saw one company where 80 percent of the top executives were new within a nine-month period. Most of the new managers were concerned primarily with short term objectives. They were afraid they wouldn't be there for another twelve months if they didn't get ahead on the political side very, very quickly. That is not a good environment for installing MRP.

I look for a company that is very people-oriented. Somehow MRP seems to fit very well into a company like that because it is basically a set of tools to help people do their jobs better. I look for a company where they understand fundamentals of management like how to establish objectives and accountability even before they have MRP. Once they have the more powerful tools, a company like this will be able to get a lot better results than a company that doesn't know how to manage well.

MRP is certainly not a substitute for management in any way. The best environment for successful MRP is a well managed company. Professionals, given better tools to work with, can get unbelievable results. At the Chair Plant of Steelcase, where they produce over 20,000 chairs a week, 2,000 customer orders, they have been on schedule 233 out of 234 consecutive weeks. (If I had told them that was possible when they were implementing MRP, they would have laughed at me!) At the Cameron Iron Works plant in Leeds, England, they are getting excellent results from MRP and their plant manager said to their executive vice president, "Ollie Wight is a lousy salesman. When you do it well, it's a lot better than he describes it." At Abbott Laboratories in Canada, they wrote an article in which they understandably bragged about the fact that they were hitting their master schedule 96 percent of the time. By the time the article got published, they had hit it 100 percent for three consecutive weeks. The **results in a well-managed company will be beyond their expectations,** from my experience.

Chapter 7

How Do We Implement MRP II?

Exec   You've told us **what** has to be done. Now let's talk about **how** to do it. How do we implement it?

OW   There are six basic steps in implementation:

1. The first-cut education.
2. The justification.
3. Picking a full time project leader.
4. Professional guidance.
5. Making up a project plan and establishing accountability for the elements in that plan.
6. A regular management review.

Exec   Who would be involved in that first-cut education?

OW   The purpose of the first-cut education is to prepare some key people to do a justification, so only a few people should be involved. We recommend sending the following to the Top Management Class:

1. Chief Executive Officer (General Manager or President usually).
2. Vice President of Manufacturing.
3. Vice President of Finance.
4. Vice President of Engineering.
5. Vice President of Marketing.
6. Vice President of Administration.
7. Vice President of Human Resources.

Then we recommend sending the following people — primarily their counterparts one level down — to the five-day class (all of these classes are described in the reference section at the back of the book):

1. Plant Manager.
2. Materials Manager.
3. Purchasing Manager.
4. Accounting Manager.
5. Engineering Manager.
6. Marketing Manager.

7. Systems Manager.
8. Personnel Manager.

Exec   You've told us about results and costs, do you have any hints on handling the justification?

OW   Well, as I mentioned, we use the cost of money in looking at the return on an inventory reduction. If two million dollars is estimated to be the potential inventory reduction, we would probably use a number like 15 percent, assuming that the cost of money will vary between 10 and 20 percent over the next few years. That would amount to $300,000 a year. For customer service, we normally look at what additional business — not due to increased normal growth — due to better customer service would be anticipated. If sales were expected to increase by 2 million dollars, for example, then 10 percent of that, or $200,000 would be the number that we would usually use as a pretax return. This, again, is conservative for most companies, especially since it represents incremental business. Productivity is usually estimated by figuring the number of people in assembly and subassembly areas, multiplying that by the costs to keep them on the payroll (salary plus out-of-pocket fringes, etc.) and attaching a percentage figure to that. Nonassembly areas are usually calculated separately because they represent a smaller percentage of productivity improvement. We don't usually put anything in for the productivity improvement to be anticipated from having more of the foreman's time available to do his job. But management should recognize that the potential exists and should set high expectations for improved cost reduction, etc. because the foreman does have that time available when the firefighting is dramatically reduced. The purchased material savings area is pretty straightforward. The return is typically about 5 percent of the total purchased cost in companies where more time available to the people can result in cost reductions. I don't think there are any other particular hints to give you in the area of costs that haven't already been covered.

Exec   Okay, what about this project leader?

OW   This is one of the classic places where people seem to be magnetically attracted to making the wrong turn. There are four major mistakes that I've seen made:

1. Picking a data processing or systems person as project leader. This violates that principle of accountability.

2. Hiring an MRP "expert" from outside of the company to be the project leader. Not that a person like this couldn't be part of the project team, but it's much easier to teach a person who knows your company, your products, and your people about MRP than it is to teach an MRP "expert" about your company, your products, and your people. Take one of your own people who has a high level of credibility within the company and a good deal of experience.

3. Picking a "lightweight." One company picked a young man just out of college to be the project leader. He was a fine person with plenty of potential, but his credibility with the people, like first-line supervision, was nonexistent. Once again, management saw MRP as a computer system and assigned him to the project because he had a degree in computer science!

4. Making the job of installing MRP a part-time project for the project leader. Unfortunately, the day-to-day firefighting will always take precedence and it will take forever to install a system.

Exec   Ollie, you sound pretty hard-nosed about the right and wrong way to go about this.

OW   I know what works. You're playing a game that includes both odds and stakes. The stakes are very high. While few companies "fail" with MRP in terms of having a real disaster, most companies need the results and most CEOs will be measured on achieving them. What do they do for an encore? The problems won't go away or get easier. They've already got people who are skeptical, and some who are even cynical about anything that even smacks of the computer. If they don't make it as Class A or B this time, it'll be a long time before they get another chance. The stakes are simply too high to take any chances. The odds can be made just about 100 percent for success. There's a way to do it right. It˜ been proven. People who take the short cuts are exposing themselves to risks that **appear reasonable only to the inexperienced.**

Exec   What about the area of professional guidance? We talked about the cost of consulting before, but how can we be sure we are getting a competent consultant? Most of us have had the experience of hiring a consultant who left us with a lot of flow charts and notebooks, but not much else.

OW   This certainly is an area where it's easy to make a mistake. I personally don't agree with the philosophy of most large consulting firms. I think it's all wrong for the following reasons:

1. They want to **do it for you** because the more people they rent out to you, the more money they make.

2. Most of their people are technical people. Thus, their concentration is on the **"system"** — the least significant part of the project. Not that it doesn't have to be done right, but it's the management part of MRP that's the tough part. It's making the transition from the world of the informal system to the world of the formal system. And most consulting firms have very few people who can contribute much in this critical area.

3. Because they make money renting bodies, they love to reinvent the wheel; this is not the way to keep a system standard and simple. Usually, the system turns out to be **theirs,** not **yours.** You'd be far better off to get their best man to come in once every four to six weeks, rather than have that person

sell you the job and "supervise it" while a bunch of inexperienced people learn at your expense.

4. The excuse of some of these consultants is that just being the catalyst won't work for many companies because they "need more help than that." Yes, that's often true. But the help they need is not in the systems area where the consultants have the most competence, but in the management area where they, for the most part, are ill-qualified to help. Not that these consultants aren't sincere, but most of them still think that the "system" will do it. That's one of the reasons that they have such an awful track record for client success. No system can substitute for good management. If management isn't capable of installing MRP without a lot of "hand-holding," their chances of being able to manage with MRP after it is installed are slim indeed. The track record of consulting proves that.

It's up to you to check the consultant out. I know consultants who've written books, who give talks, and who are well known in our field. But finding their successful clients would be extremely challenging. If a consultant or educator cannot show you where they have clients who are successful as a result of the consultant's assistance, that person should not be used in your MRP project. Check their credentials. Don't believe what they tell you without talking to their clients and proving, to your own satisfaction, that they have the competence to help you.

Exec   That makes sense. What is the "project plan"?

OW   We've made a generalized implementation plan based on the experiences of companies that have installed MRP successfully. It goes into the steps of implementation like fixing inventory records, bills of material, and education in considerable detail; and it shows the sequence of the important elements in installing an MRP II system. It's included in this book after the section on references. Use it to make your own project plan.

Plagiarize it. Cross off the items that don't apply to your company, add in a few that do, if there are any. It's a road map for doing MRP successfully that's been used by a great many companies and should be a great help to your company.

Exec   Just what exactly do you mean here by "accountability"?

OW   Every element of the project plan should have a name and a time attached to it. The person on the project team should be accountable for getting this accomplished. Some people will be on the project team full time, typically a few people from engineering, for example, who are fixing bills of material, systems people, etc. Others, like people from accounting, may only have to be participating part-time. But they should have specific assignments and be held accountable for accomplishing them. And you know whose name should be at the top of the project plan, don't you? The CEO. This isn't just another ploy to make the CEO's life tough. It's already tough. But, in the event the company spends a half a million to three-quarters of a million dollars installing an MRP system, and it doesn't produce results, you can be sure that the CEO will be held responsible. It's good to start right out with that person's name on the top of the project plan so people know that this is not another data processing exercise, but is a serious business project and that management is providing the leadership.

Exec   How often must management review the project?

OW   Every two weeks or so the management steering committee, consisting of the CEO and the top executives from each of the major functions, should review the project plan to see what is being done, what tasks are in trouble, and what needs to be done to get the project back on the track. This should be taken as seriously as if a new plant were being built. In fact, I've been through building new plants and installing MRP II and, frankly, MRP II is more challenging. Not that it can't be done, but it cannot be approached cavalierly as a computer project if you expect to get results.

Exec   I'm a little nervous about how we convert to a new system like MRP II without totally upsetting the company and running the risk of getting into serious trouble, at least at the very beginning. How do we accomplish this?

OW   There are three fundamental ways of converting to MRP:

1. The **"cold turkey"** approach says, "Pull the big switch Monday, and put MRP II on the air across the board." This is irresponsible. No company should ever use this approach. Only a few companies have done it successfully, and every one of them that I talk to recommends against other companies using that approach. One company said, "It almost did us in." Other companies **have** been done in by the cold turkey approach. They overwhelmed their people and they never did get the results they should have from MRP.

2. Running systems in **"parallel"** doesn't work for MRP because MRP is a system that couldn't be done manually. Therefore, manual systems that are now on the computer can not be used in parallel with MRP because they will produce conflicting information.

3. The **"pilot"** approach is ill-understood by most people. They want to know, "What product line should we pick?" "Should it be the easiest one?" "Should it be the most difficult one?" "How will we know whether it's working in the factory when we don't have valid need dates on everything, only the items in the pilot?" None of these questions are valid. The issues are to pick a **person,** not a product — the most enthusiastic, hardworking planner in the company, the one that is most likely to make MRP work. Then check to make sure that he understands the system and is able to operate without a shortage list. That means the material requirements planning pilot is working.

Exec   How do we know whether we're ready to go on the air with the MRP pilot or not?

OW   Inventory records should be 95 percent accurate using cycle counting as a measure. Cycle counting is done daily on a sample group of items. If 100 items are counted, and 95 out of 100 percent are within a reasonable counting tolerance, that is 95 percent inventory record accuracy. Experience shows that without this level of accuracy, data integrity will be a real problem in making MRP work. Ninety-eight to 99 percent of the bills of material should be 100 percent accurate. Ninety-five to 98 percent of the routings should be 100 percent accurate. Seventy-five to 80 percent of the people should have at least some degree of education before the pilot is even started with 100 percent of the people as a final goal. These are the most critical areas.

Exec   What's a reasonable time schedule for installing MRP?

OW   I like to see my clients put the **pilot** material requirements planning system on the air in nine to twelve months. I like to see them have all of material requirements planning on the air in another three months. All of capacity planning, shop floor control, vendor scheduling, and accounting should be working in another three months. That's a fifteen to eighteen month period of time.

Exec   Wow! That's an ambitious schedule. How can a project this big be accomplished that fast?

OW   In Chapter 4 and Chapter 6, we discussed the technical, data, and people areas that need to be handled to make MRP work. The time-consuming elements of an MRP system are:

1. **Technical** — development and implementation of the software and systems.

2. **Data** — bills of material, inventory records, and routings.

3. **People** — education.

These are the items in the critical path. If it looks like MRP is going to take more than eighteen months, they should be reviewed to see what can be done to shorten up the time.

Exec   Why are you so adamant about doing this on such a tight time schedule?

OW   There are two very good reasons. If you take an extra year to install MRP and the system has been justified based on an annual savings of one million dollars a year, the extra year will cost you one million dollars that you'll never have another chance to recover. But even more important is the problem of the span of attention of people from management right on down. As I told you earlier, MRP requires dedication and especially **enthusiasm** on the part of everyone. Keeping that enthusiasm at a high peak, and running the business at the same time with all the normal problems of manufacturing like hitting schedules, customer problems, competitive problems, labor problems, government regulations from OSHA and the FDA for example, environment problems, product liability problems, etc. is tough. The odds against maintaining that level of enthusiasm for much over two years are staggering. Companies that plan MRP to take a long time and make the installation schedules nice and "comfortable" will probably still be installing MRP six years from now and aren't very likely to ever see the real success that management can achieve from these better tools.

Chapter 8

How Do We Manage with MRP II?

Exec   What's really different about managing using MRP II?

OW   With MRP II, the CEO is responsible for:

1. Establishing objectives.

2. Establishing accountability.

3. **Making the production plan.**

4. Making sure that the plan is valid, that the data is correct, that the master schedule represents what's really going to be built.

5. Establishing policy on subjects like master scheduling.

6. Making sure that every member of the management team uses the system rather than "end-running" it. It is a new set of tools and people will instinctively come up with excuses for not using it like, "But we needed that order out in a real hurry." In a good MRP system, there is no reason why the order can't be delivered just as quickly as it could if end-running the system, and with a lot more knowledge of what the consequences will be.

7. Measuring performance against valid plans.

8. Measuring people on their execution of the plans.

9. Getting rid of the adversary relationships and getting people to work together as a team far better than was possible before.

Exec   Wait a minute. Back up here. Does the CEO really have to **make** the production plan?

OW   The production plan is a production rate for a product family usually expressed in units. Companies have many production plans for their different product families. The production plan starts by looking at current backlog for a make-to-order product or current inventory for a make-to-stock product. If the sales & operations plan was being made for one year in the future, for example, the desired change in ending backlog or inventory would be added to or subtracted from the sales forecast for the product family to determine the production rate required. Sales & operations plans are often made a year or two in advance, broken down into quarters and months, and then reviewed monthly. At the monthly meeting, the top operating executive should bring together the top marketing, manufacturing, finance, and engineering people to establish these sales & operations plans. Whether the top executive does the actual calculations is unimportant. The point is that with a closed loop MRP system and MRP II, top level planning can be translated right down to the detail level, and it's extremely important that the top level planning be done properly.

Exec   And you say this is **my** responsibility, Ollie?

OW   Absolutely. It's been said that there are three conflicting objectives in a manufacturing company: maximum customer service, minimum inventory, and maximum plant efficiency. These objectives have to be reconciled to come up with reasonable plans. These plans will determine the levels of inventory, the levels of production and, as a consequence, will determine cash flow, return on investment, etc. The tools are here now so that management can get results from better planning. But it's up to management to do that better planning. They now have a great deal more control over their own destinies.

Exec   Okay, Ollie, that's a new perspective. You know the rest of what you say doesn't really sound like anything new. It just sounds like good management. Aren't you talking about "management by objectives"?

OW   Management by objectives (MBO) to me is just common sense. I don't see anything startling about it. Perhaps that is what's so great about it. As I understand it, it all started when Peter Drucker said, "Let's spend less time worrying about what we are doing, and more time worrying about what we are trying to accomplish." I guess all good things are simple in retrospect. Yes, MRP II and MBO go hand in hand. In fact, I don't know how MBO could really work in a manufacturing environment without the valid plans that MRP II makes possible. I believe that MRP II is a prerequisite to effective MBO. One of the reasons why MBO has not produced all of the results it should have in the past was that, once again, people assumed that things worked the way they should in a factory and didn't recognize that valid plans simply didn't exist. On the other hand, now that the more professional tools are here, the "MBO" approach — if you want to call it that — **must** be used to make it really work.

Exec   Do we really have **different** objectives with MRP II than we did before?

OW   Yes, especially in the area of inventory record accuracy, bills of material, the master schedule; and now we spell out objectives and establish accountability where we really didn't before. Now we have line accountability for inventory accuracy, for example, and measure managers on performance against this objective. One company I know has a "logistics group" that reports to marketing that generates the master schedule. At first, this sounds frightening. But, in fact, the marketing group has the objectives of keeping plant employment at a level rate and providing a doable plan. As long as they have those objectives, there's no reason why marketing can't make valid plans for manufacturing. I worked in a company once where 80 percent of the business came in from branch warehouses that reported to marketing. It was a disaster. In a highly seasonal business, they virtually shut the factory down during the off season and ordered everything in sight during the peak season without accepting any responsibility for keeping the plant operating at a level rate. But that was the fault of management, not the fault of marketing. It's management's responsibility to set the proper objectives, and translate these objectives into higher level planning through the production plans. With the tools we have today, these higher level plans can be translated into valid plans right down through the organization.

Exec   The more you think about MRP II, the more sense it makes. It really is a way to eliminate a lot of today's frustration and confusion.

OW   It definitely is. Consider a company that had three assembly plants all drawing from one fabrication plant. The fabrication plant manager was always in trouble because whenever something wasn't shipped, the assembly plants could produce a shortage list that showed that the missing items were **"past due"** from the fabrication plant. Of course they were! With order launching and expediting, virtually everything was "past due." Another company has a working MRP system. They have a fabrication plant manager and an assembly plant manager. But their fabrication plant manager isn't constantly in trouble. He has a valid schedule. As long as he works to that schedule, the right material will be made and assembly can meet their schedule. In the world of the informal system, there was always confusing, conflicting information. In the world of MRP II, plans should make sense, they should be attainable, and if each member of the team executes his plans, the company objectives will be met.

Exec   Ollie, doesn't management have to formalize some things that weren't really spelled out before?

OW   Yes, like written policies for things like the sales & operations plan and the master schedule. These weren't particularly significant before, but now they are. Wouldn't it be interesting, for example, to have manufacturing write down their understanding of how far out the master schedule ought to be held firm and not changed, except for a real crisis, and marketing's ideas about this same kind of policy — and what constituted a **real** crisis! We would, undoubtedly, get a very different set of answers. And this kind of policy needs to be worked out ahead of time, answering some fundamental questions. How often must the forecast be reviewed? How often will a sales & operations planning meeting take place? Who will attend it? Who will be responsible for what input to the sales & operations plan? How will it be measured? Who will sign off on the sales & operations plan? When can changes be made in the master schedule? We need some guidelines for knowing when changes can be made quite readily and when they'll have to be checked to see if they are doable. One company, for example, makes any change within the first four weeks subject to approval by the vice president of manufacturing, any in the next four weeks by the director of materials management, and beyond that, the master scheduler can make the changes. In the past, we didn't have the tools to execute these policies in a methodical way. Now we have the tools and it's management's responsibility to get people together to spell out these policies. It's important to establish the ground rules before the ball goes into play, rather than debating the ground rules constantly after the ball is in play.

Exec   And management must set the example for keeping the numbers right?

OW   Yes. That was something that wasn't particularly important before. I sent a young man down to Black and Decker many years ago to see their MRP system. He was a very perceptive person. His reaction was, "Everything impressed me, but what impressed me the most was their immense respect for numbers." The pilot who flies by instruments has an immense respect for numbers!

Exec   You talked about some of the things we had to measure before we implemented the system, like inventory record accuracy, bills of material, and routings. How will we measure the system after it goes on the air?

OW   We will have to measure these on a continuing basis. We can measure bills of material by counting the number of times the assembly department, for example, has to go back to the stockroom to get material because of a bill of material error. If 100 bills were issued in a week and one error was reported, that's 99 percent.

Routings will be measured by feedback from the daily shop schedule that we call a "dispatch report." If a job is in the department but doesn't show on the dispatch report, or vice versa, it will have to be checked out. If this is due to a routing error and two are discovered during a week when 100 routings were issued, that's a 98 percent routing accuracy. Other elements that need to be measured are:

The master schedule. Typically, companies take a "snapshot" of it once a month and then measure what percentage of the individual items were actually made. They then find out why the items in the master schedule weren't made. Identifying the causes of the problems, and fixing them, is part of execution.

Shipping dollars. This is usually already measured in most companies today.

Delivery performance. Most companies measure this in one way or another and should continue to.

Schedules. Output in standard hours by work center should be measured against the capacity plan. Shop, vendor, and engineering orders and projects completed on schedule against the total orders promised for a given time period should be measured.

Forecasts. I'm not really terribly concerned about how forecasts are measured, as long as we measure them some way because everything that's measured tends to improve.

Of course, the essence of good control is to audit and find out what's actually causing the problems and what has to be done to improve performance. The measurement doesn't do that — it simply identifies the fact that there are problems.

One of the key measures, in my opinion, is the shortage list. The reason this is such a powerful measure is that we can use it to track down the causes of the shortages to find out why they are happening. In fact, if you are really operating MRP II at a Class A level, there **should not be a shortage list.**

Exec   **No** shortage list? Can people really make that happen?

OW   Why not? MRP is just a simulation of the shortage list. If it's being used properly to prevent the shortages, there's no reason to have a shortage list. But one of the important messages for management to get across is that MRP is not going to make that happen, **people** are going to make it happen. Whatever you do, **don't fire your expeditor** when you put in MRP! Too many people get the impression that somehow we just won't have to exert the effort with MRP, and that simply isn't true. There won't be as many crises — that's for sure. But there will still be the vendor that has scrap at the last minute, the quality problem that shows up in assembly, and that's when a company will need the same kind of "can do" spirit they had before. People will have to exert the same kind of effort they do to **fix** the shortages now, and use it to **prevent** the shortages with MRP. Steelcase, for example, still flies an occasional part in. The difference is that they do it far less than ever before and they do it in order to hit the schedule 100 percent!

Exec   Okay, Ollie, you make a good point. The real results are going to come from the execution of MRP. Have MRP users learned anything about execution — making it happen — beyond just "good management"?

OW   One of the approaches that we have found to be very helpful is to list each manager's top ten problems. You know the old 80/20 rule, the vital few, and the trivial many? Identify these problems, have the manager sign off on what the solutions are and when they will be accomplished, and then measure the manager's performance in solving these problems correctly and on time.

Exec   And the emphasis with MRP II is on teamwork, isn't it? Everyone has to play his position.

OW Yes, and you know we've talked about teamwork for years to the point where many people are sick of hearing about it. But we were missing that vital link — valid plans. Plans, obviously, won't make teamwork happen; management must do that. But even the most dedicated management is going to have trouble getting real teamwork without the game plan to do it. MRP II is that game plan.

Exec And you say if we do install MRP II properly, MRP II will work — I mean MRP will give **us** the tools so that we can get the results?

OW Every time. Without fail. There is a right way to implement MRP II, and if you do it properly, it will work. You talked about the "failures" earlier. Take a look at the people who didn't succeed and look at the way they approached it. Find out who their project manager was. Where did they put the emphasis? Did they do the right education job? Inevitably, you'll find that they approached it as a computer system, not a people system. They didn't recognize that it was a new, more professional way to run a manufacturing business made possible by some tools that were made possible by the computer.

Exec Okay, Ollie, what's your forecast for the future? How is management of a manufacturing company going to be changing as a result of these tools?

OW I see a number of changes taking place:

1. There will be a lot more emphasis on managing a manufacturing business as a **profession**. This is vital not only to our economy, but to our society.

2. We will put a lot more emphasis on establishing the proper objectives and measuring performance rather than the "organizationitis" that many companies use today in the hopes of somehow "osmoting" the right objectives to the right part of the company. I don't care if the stockroom reports to the personnel department as long as the person-

nel manager is held accountable for getting material out to the shop floor, keeping records accurate, etc.

3. I think we've got the gee whiz days of the computer behind us. I think we've learned from the school of hard knocks not just in the MRP area, but in many other areas. Now our real emphasis has to be on **using** these tools — not as an end in themselves — but as a way to enhance our capabilities in utilizing the most important resources we have in our manufacturing industries, our **human resources.**

References

Sources for Additional Information

Preparing yourself to implement a Class A MRP II system requires careful study of a huge amount of information, far more than could be included in this or any other book. The Oliver Wight Companies can provide further assistance in getting ready, including books on the subject and live education.

Oliver Wight Publications, Inc.

Oliver Wight Publications, Inc. was created in 1981 to publish books on planning and scheduling, written by leading educators and consultants in the field.

A complete library of books on Manufacturing Resource Planning, Just-in-Time, and Distribution Resource Planning are available.

For more information, or to order publications, contact:

Oliver Wight Publications, Inc.
5 Oliver Wight Drive
Essex Junction, VT 05452
800-343-0625 or 802-878-8161

Oliver Wight Education Associates

OWEA is made up of a group of independent MRP II educators and consultants around the world who share a common philosophy and common goals. Classes directed towards both upper- and middle-level management are being taught in various locations around the U.S. and Canada, as well as abroad. For a detailed class brochure, listing course descriptions, instructors, costs, dates, and locations, or for the name of a recommended consultant in your area, please contact:

Oliver Wight Education Associates
P.O. Box 435
Newbury, NH 03255
800-258-3862 or 603-763-5926

Oliver Wight Video Productions, Inc.

The Oliver Wight Video Library offers companies the video-based materials they need to teach the "critical mass" of their employees about the principles of MRP II and Just-in-Time. For more information on obtaining the Oliver Wight Video Library, contact:

Oliver Wight Video Productions, Inc.
5 Oliver Wight Drive
Essex Junction, VT 05452
800-343-0625 or 802-878-8161

The Implementation Plan

This implementation plan was developed by Darryl Landvater, President of Oliver Wight Video Productions, Inc. It has been updated to include the financial functions that would be included in an MRP II system. In its earlier form, it has been used by hundreds of companies as a road map for implementing MRP successfully.

The Proven Path

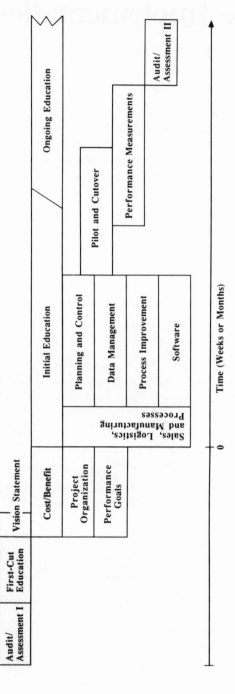

MRP II Detailed Implementation Plan

More and more people are asking for information on the implementation and operation of MRP systems. These people are not interested in being sold on MRP. MRP systems work. The proof is available and companies are using them every day. People who understand the fundamentals and the logical simplicity of MRP are looking for a proven way to implement the system.

This detailed implementation plan is a road map to help people implement MRP systems. The implementation plan outlines the basic functional areas needed to implement MRP. These functional areas are then broken down into specific milestones. This listing of broad functional areas and specific tasks provides a very practical plan.

PEOPLE USING MRP

The implementation plan is also meant for companies using an MRP system. There are many companies which have the technical part of an MRP system in place. Yet, they are not using the system well. The implementation plan can help these companies. The jobs in improving an MRP system are the same as the jobs to implement it correctly. The only difference is that some of these jobs may have already been done. If so, they can be deleted from the plan.

MRP II

MRP, which started out over ten years ago as a better way to order material, has evolved into MRP II. MRP II is a total company-wide system. It is a way to get all the people in the company working to the same game plan; to the same set of numbers. A company can now plan material, capacity, finance, marketing strategy, etc. all with the same system. In addition, all these things can be simulated to provide the management of the company with real planning capability.

This version of the implementation plan includes the steps for MRP II.

Finally, the implementation plan has been put on video tape. The course MRP II: Making It Work available from Oliver Wight Video Productions, Inc., uses this implementation plan as the core of the section on implementing MRP. Each of the points in this implementation plan are expanded significantly and explained in that video course.

USING THE PLAN

The implementation plan is a generalized framework applicable to nearly any company. Its two primary uses are:

1. To provide a clear statement of priorities — to separate the vital and trivial, and keep them in perspective.

2. To provide a road map for implementation.

The implementation plan is organized to constantly focus attention on the items that have the greatest impact on the potential for success. The people part of an MRP system is fully 80 percent of the system. The system will only work when people understand what it is, how it works, and what their responsibilities are. For this reason, the education and training are listed at the front of the implementation plan. The computer software and programming effort is not as likely to be something which prevents the success of an MRP system, and so this topic is covered later in the plan.

The other purpose is to provide a detailed schedule of events that have to be accomplished in order to implement the system. The most effective way to use the plan is to tailor the plan to each company and then use it as the agenda for management reviews of implementation progress.

PRACTICALITY

This implementation plan is not a theoretical exercise. In the six years since the first version of the plan was developed, it has been used successfully by a number of companies. Whether these companies would have been successful without the plan, I cannot say. But it does work, it is practical, and those who have used it swear by it.

TAILORING THE PLAN TO YOUR COMPANY

The implementation plan is a general framework stated in terms of departments and job titles. The departments and job titles should be replaced by the names of the people within the organization who will be responsible for the tasks.

The implementation plan also contains an approximate time frame for scheduling the tasks under each of the functional topics. The scheduled due dates for the tasks in implementation are given under the heading "DATE." These due dates were developed based on the dependence of some tasks on others. The times on the plan, +3 and +7 for example, are months relative to a starting point. A time of +3 means the task should be completed three months after the start date. The start date used in the plan is the date that formal commitment is given to the project.

The plan should be rewritten to include calendar dates in place of the scheduled completion dates in months. Columns should also be added for the scheduled start date, the actual start date, and the actual completion date. The scheduled start dates are not on the generalized plan since the size of the different tasks will vary from company to company. The actual start date and actual completion date should be included on the plan to indicate the progress or lack of it during the management reviews of implementation.

The comments column on the implementation plan is meant to give a short explanation of the phases of the plan and tasks that make up each phase. Some people choose to leave these explanations in the final version of the plan, others leave them out. In either case, additional comments on the progress of the tasks should also be included as the plan is periodically updated. These comments would indicate, for example, the results of the cycle counts, or any other information about one of the items in the plan.

A company may also have to add or delete tasks from the implementation plan to account for situations that are a part of the implementation, or work that has already been done. As an example of an item that would be deleted from the plan, a company may have already enclosed the stockrooms and may have started cycle counting. In this case, it makes no sense to count 100 parts as a starting point. As an example of an item that would have to be added to the plan, a company may have to convert to a different computer to do MRP. In this case, the conversion from one computer to the other should be included on the detailed implementation plan.

Figure 1 is an example of the implementation plan before and after it has been tailored to a company. This example includes replacement of departments and job titles with people's names, the inclusion of calendar dates with columns for scheduling dates, and some comments on tasks that are working.

MRP II
Proven Path Detailed Implementation Plan

TASK	RESPONSIBLE	COMMENTS
1. AUDIT/ASSESSMENT I	Top Mgmt. Middle Mgmt.	Assess the company's current situation. In most cases, this is done with the help of an outside consultant with Class A credentials.
2. FIRST-CUT EDUCATION	Top Mgmt. Middle Mgmt.	What is MRP II, how does it work, why should a company commit to it? Top management should attend the Top Management Course, key middle managers should attend the Five-Day Course, Executive Torchbearer and Team Leader should attend Successful Implementation Class.
3. VISION STATEMENT	Top Mgmt. Middle Mgmt.	A short, concise document defining what we want to accomplish, and when it should be in place.
4. COST/BENEFIT	Top Mgmt. Middle Mgmt.	A clear listing of the costs and benefits, agreed to by the key players.
A. Prepare cost/benefit.	Top Mgmt. Middle Mgmt.	Cost/benefit analysis.
B. Commit to implementation.	Top Mgmt.	Approve the implementation. Communicate the commitment. Deliver clear, consistent messages.
5. PROJECT ORGANIZATION	Top Mgmt.	Create the appropriate management and operational teams.
A. Executive Steering Committee.	Top Mgmt.	Include designation of Executive Torchbearer. Schedule review meetings once a month.
B. Project Team.	Top Mgmt.	Team Leader should be full-time.
C. Outside counsel.	Top Mgmt.	Outside consultant with Class A experience.
D. Spin-off task groups.	Ex. Steering Committee	Identify initial groups, more may be needed later.
6. PERFORMANCE GOALS	Top Mgmt. Middle Mgmt.	Using the ABCD Checklist, agree on expected performance levels and measurements.

MRP II
Proven Path Detailed Implementation Plan

TASK	RESPONSIBLE	COMMENTS
7. INITIAL EDUCATION	Team Leader	Provide the necessary understanding to all people who will be designing and using the new tools.
A. Outside education for people who will be leaders at the in-house series of business meetings and key managers.	Team Leader	To be effective discussion leaders, these managers need exposure at either the Top Management Course or the Five-Day Course. The key managers mentioned here are people critical to the design or operation, but who have not been covered under first-cut education and who are not leaders for the business meetings.
B. Outside education for people designated as in-house experts.	Team Leader	Generally, in-house experts are designated in the following areas: Manufacturing Strategy, Sales & Operations Planning, Master Production Scheduling, Material Requirements Planning, Capacity Management and Shop Scheduling, Purchasing, Inventory Record Accuracy, Bill of Material Accuracy, and Financial Integration. These in-house experts may or may not be part of the project team.
C. Project Team/Discussion Leaders video course.	Team Leader	A series of business meetings where the general principles are translated into the specifics of operation for your company. Acquire the MRP II Video Library.
D. Top Management video course.	Executive Torchbearer/ Project Leader	A series of business meetings where the top managers apply the concepts to their company.
E. Mixed Management Overview video course.	Discussion Leaders	A series of business meetings covering the overview materials, with a mixed group of managers from each of the different functional areas. The objectives are to understand the concepts, to better understand one another, and to help in team building.

MRP II
Proven Path Detailed Implementation Plan

TASK	RESPONSIBLE	COMMENTS
F. Department specific video courses.	Discussion Leaders	Series of business meetings organized by department. The objectives are to determine specifically what changes need to be made to run the business differently in these departments. Typical groups for these meetings include, but are not limited to: Production and Inventory Control, Purchasing, Manufacturing Supervision, Quality, Sales and Marketing, Engineering, Finance, Management Information Systems, Personnel, Stockroom, Group Leaders, and Direct Labor Employees.
8. SALES, LOGISTICS, AND MANUFACTURING PRO-CESSES	Top Mgmt. Middle Mgmt.	Develop a detailed statement of how these processes will operate following implementation. The Project Team/Discussion Leaders series of business meetings (Task #7C above) generally provides most of the information needed for this task. Key issues or changes should be approved by top management.

MRP II
Proven Path Detailed Implementation Plan

TASK	RESPONSIBLE	COMMENTS
9. PLANNING AND CONTROL PROCESSES		Identification of the systems necessary for effective planning and control. Some of these systems will be implemented using the pilot approach.
A. Sales & Operations Planning.	Top Mgmt.	Can be started right away. Format, policies, unit of measure, and family designations can be developed in the first few meetings and revised as needed thereafter.
B. Demand Management.	Sales Mgr.	Focus on improving the demand side of the business through: sales planning, item forecasting, eliminating or reducing detailed forecasting wherever possible by using DRP or interfacing with customer scheduling systems.
C. Master Production Scheduling.	P&IC Mgr.	Decisions on what level in the product structure to master schedule, and what items will be master scheduled. Typically started with material planning as part of the pilot.
1. Develop a master scheduling policy.	Top Mgmt. Sales & Mktg. P&IC Mfg. Suprvsn.	Should address the following: 1. Procedure for changing the master production schedule. Who can request a change, how the proposed change is investigated, and who should approve it. 2. Periodic reviews of actual production vs. the master production schedule with an emphasis on problem resolution.
D. Material Planning.	P&IC Mgr.	Begun as a pilot.
E. Capacity Planning.	P&IC Mgr. Mfg. Suprvsn.	Sometimes implementation is delayed until after master scheduling and material planning are fully implemented.

MRP II
Proven Path Detailed Implementation Plan

TASK	RESPONSIBLE	COMMENTS
F. Shop Scheduling.	P&IC Mgr. Mfg. Suprvsn.	Includes shop floor control and input-output control. Some companies today are using kanban on the factory floor in place of traditional shop floor control. Other companies are using both kanban in some areas, and traditional shop floor control in other areas.
G. Supplier Scheduling & Development	Purchasing Mgr.	Typically started as a pilot with one or several suppliers.

MRP II
Proven Path Detailed Implementation Plan

TASK	RESPONSIBLE	COMMENTS
10. DATA MANAGEMENT		These are the steps required to attain the necessary levels of data accuracy.
A. Inventory Record Accuracy.	Stockroom Mgr.	Objective is a minimum 95 percent inventory record accuracy.
1. Measure a sample as a starting point.	Stockroom Mgr.	Develop an objective assessment of the starting point. Most companies use a sample of 100 items.
2. Provide the tools for limited access and transaction recording.	Stockroom Mgr.	Includes enough stockroom people, adequate space, counting scales, and typically a fence. In the case of a simultaneous MRP II/JIT implementation, see the JIT implementation plan for the handling of point-of-use and point-of-manufacture storage. Transaction system must be simple and easy to use.
3. Implement control group cycle counting.	Stockroom Mgr.	Used to find and fix the root causes of errors.
4. Begin cycle counting all items.	Stockroom Mgr.	Done after the causes of errors have been corrected. Several approaches are commonly used: process-control cycle counting, cycle counting by ABC code, random cycle counting.
B. Bill of Material Accuracy.	Engr. Mgr. Mfg. Suprvsn.	Objective is a minimum 98 percent bill of material accuracy, and an accurate bill of material structure.
1. Measure a sample of single-level bills as a starting point.	Engr. Mgr. Mfg. Suprvsn.	Develop an objective assessment of the starting point. Most companies use a sample of 100 single-level bills.
2. Assign responsibility for bill of material accuracy.	Top Mgmt.	Working with all the different departments who are users of the bills of material.

MRP II
Proven Path Detailed Implementation Plan

TASK	RESPONSIBLE	COMMENTS
3. Verify bills of material for correct item numbers and quantity per.	Engr. Mgr. Mfg. Suprvsn.	Typically done by exception: issue to manufacturing per the bill of material and track exceptions. A cycle audit, line-by-line audit, and/or disassembly of the product can also be used where appropriate. Objective is to highlight errors and correct them as well as correcting the root causes of the errors.
4. Verify correct structure in the bills of material.	Engr. Mgr. Mfg. Suprvsn.	Typical areas of work include: 1. Representing how material moves in the factory. 2. Showing raw material on the bills of material. 3. Including modules and self-consumed assemblies where appropriate. 4. Removing unnecessary levels from the bills of material.
5. Develop and implement bill of material policies.	Engr. Mgr.	Typical policies include: 1. Engineering (or formula) change procedure. 2. Documenting new or special products. 3. Temporary material substitutions.
C. Routing Accuracy.	Mfg. Engineering Mgr.	Objective is a minimum 95 percent routing accuracy.
1. Measure 100 routings as a starting point.	Mfg. Engineering Mgr.	Develop an objective assessment of the starting point.
2. Assign responsibility for routing accuracy.	Top Mgmt.	May involve assigning areas of responsibility if these do not already exist.
3. Verify routings.	Mfg. Engr. Mgr.	Typically done by auditing work on the factory floor for: correct work center, correct operation sequence, reasonable time standard (plus or minus 10 percent).

MRP II
Proven Path Detailed Implementation Plan

TASK	RESPONSIBLE	COMMENTS
D. Item Data.	P&IC Mgr. Purchasing Mgr.	Have knowledgeable people verify this information.
1. Verify order policies.	P&IC Mgr. Purchasing Mgr.	Decide between fixed-order quantity and lot-for-lot. Dynamic-order quantity calculations are not recommended. Fix the obvious errors in order quantities, use remainder as is, work to reduce the order quantities.
2. Verify lead times.	P&IC Mgr. Purchasing Mgr.	Manufactured items: use simple, consistent scheduling rules, fix the obvious problems, work to reduce the lead times. Purchased items: use current lead times, work with suppliers to implement supplier scheduling to get out beyond the lead times.
3. Verify safety stock levels.	P&IC Mgr. Purchasing Mgr.	Applies to independent demand items consistent with master schedule policy. For dependent demand items, restrict to special circumstances only.

MRP II
Proven Path Detailed Implementation Plan

TASK	RESPONSIBLE	COMMENTS
11. PROCESS IMPROVEMENT		MRP II is a planning and control system. JIT/TQC is process improvement; changing the business to make it more efficient, more productive, and less costly through the elimination of waste.
		Companies need to do both: Plan and control their business, and change their processes to continuously improve them. For the detailed implementation plan in the area of process improvement, see the JIT/TQC Detailed Implementation Plan.

91

MRP II
Proven Path Detailed Implementation Plan

TASK	RESPONSIBLE	COMMENTS
12. SOFTWARE		
A. Select software.	MIS Mgr.	Select and implement the software to support the planning and control systems identified above.
	MIS Mgr. P&IC Mfg. Suprvsn.	Select software that meets most of the needs from a user and MIS point of view.
1. Acquire *The Standard System* book.	MIS Mgr. P&IC Mfg. Suprvsn.	Available from Oliver Wight Limited Publications, this book provides an explanation of what a typical software package should provide.
2. If needed, schedule software consulting audit.	MIS Mgr. P&IC Mfg. Suprvsn.	Helpful in situations where new software is being used or extensive modification and/or interfacing is required.
B. Evaluate systems work and acquire necessary resources.	MIS Mgr.	Includes work needed for modifications, interfacing, and temporary bridges.
C. Implement necessary modules with modifications and interfacing.	MIS Mgr.	Typical modules include: Inventory Transactions, Bills of Material, Routings, Master Production Scheduling, Material Requirements Planning, Capacity Requirements Planning, Shop Floor Control, Input-Output Control, Purchasing, Financial Integration.
D. Agree on MIS performance standards.	MIS Mgr. P&IC Mfg. Suprvsn.	Response times, on-time completion of planning run, reports, etc.

MRP II
Proven Path Detailed Implementation Plan

TASK	RESPONSIBLE	COMMENTS
13. PILOT AND CUTOVER	Team Leader Project Team Involved Users	Conversion of the current processes to the new processes using a pilot approach.
A. Complete three pilots.	Team Leader Project Team Involved Users	Pilots are: 1. Computer pilot to test the software. 2. Conference room pilot to test procedures and people's understanding. 3. Live pilot to test the new processes and verify they are working. Systems that are typically implemented using the pilot approach are: 1. Master Production Scheduling. 2. Material Requirements Planning. 3. Shop Floor Control. 4. Supplier Scheduling and Development.
B. Monitor critical measurements.	Team Leader	Before moving into cutover, verify that the new processes and systems are working.
C. Group remaining products into several groups.	P&IC Involved Users	Three or four groups are typical.
D. Bring each group onto the new systems.	P&IC	Each group will require intense planner coverage to get them settled down.

93

TASK	RESPONSIBLE	COMMENTS
14. PERFORMANCE MEASURE-MENTS	Dept. Heads	Compare actual results to the previously agreed-upon key measurements. Typical performance measurements include: 1. Production Plan performance. 2. Master Production Schedule performance. 3. Manufacturing Schedule performance. 4. Engineering Schedule performance. 5. Supplier Delivery performance. Other measurements include: 1. Customer Service. 2. Quality. 3. Cost. 4. Velocity.
15. AUDIT/ASSESSMENT II	Top Mgmt. Middle Mgmt.	Re-assess the company's situation. Where are the current opportunities, what needs to be done next. This could be a phase 2 of the implementation, a concentrated effort to improve current levels of performance, etc. In most cases, this is done with the help of an outside consultant with Class A credentials.
16. ONGOING EDUCATION	Dept. Heads	Run a continuing program of outside education and business meetings to improve skill levels and company operating results.
A. Educate key managers new to the business.	Top Mgmt.	New managers in key positions need exposure at either the Top Management Course or Five-Day Course to continue achieving full operating benefits.

MRP II
Proven Path Detailed Implementation Plan

TASK	RESPONSIBLE	COMMENTS
B. Maintain in-house experts.	Dept. Heads	Also important to continue achieving full operating benefits.
C. Continue the series of business meetings.	Dept. Heads	These meetings focus on how to improve the operating results of the business through the use of these tools. It's good to stand back and look at the situation from time to time. Sometimes new people are run through a special series of meetings, more typically, they are included in the ongoing series of business meetings.

Excerpts from The Oliver Wight ABCD Checklist

The *Oliver Wight ABCD Checklist for Operational Excellence* is designed to help your organization assess its performance across five key areas. One area includes the essential Planning and Control Process. You can evaluate your company's planning and control operations by responding to each of the following questions and rating your company across 22 performance measures. An average total response rating of 3.5 or higher means that your company is operating at the "Class A" level of performance; a score of 2.5 to 3.49 qualifies for Class B level; an average score of 1.5 to 2.49 is a Class C level; and an average of less than 1.5 indicates a Class D level.

INTRODUCTION

Perspective

Are we doing the right things? How well are we doing them? Are we on the right track to world-class performance? It's hard to imagine three more valuable questions for all managers to ask frequently. The answers reflect current levels of performance and reveal significant opportunities for improvement.

Finding the right answers, however, requires many more questions. This checklist raises those questions. As such, it's an important tool in appraising a company's effectiveness in utilizing the many technologies available to manufacturing companies today.

A good checklist does more than tell you where you are today—it helps managers focus on what's required to become more competitive and achieve world-class levels of performance. Periodic use of the checklist generates a consistent means of assessing progress. In addition, it identifies problems early, which allow the correction process to start immediately. Further, by comparing performance against established benchmarks, people are motivated to work in a more effective manner.

Evolution

Ollie Wight created our first ABCD Checklist in 1977. It consisted of twenty items designed to evaluate a Manufacturing Resource Planning system, MRP II. The items were grouped into three categories: technical, to determine whether the design was proper; data accuracy, to determine how reliable the information was; and operational, to determine how well MRP II was understood and used within the company.

A few years later the original list was expanded to twenty-five items. This checklist is the accepted industry standard for measuring MRP II. By responding to these items, a person can objectively grade a company's use of MRP II into one of four categories: A, B, C, or D. These levels of potential have served as challenging goals, especially to reach the Class A level.

No Longer Just MRP II

During the 1980s, the third generation of the ABCD Checklist was created, which was broader in scope. It covered not only operational planning and control processes—MRP II and Distribution Resource Planning (DRP)—but also contained items in the important areas of strategic planning and Continuous Improvement. The third edition also contained entries for both the overview level, to facilitate review by the general manager and staff, and the detail level, to serve as a tool for operating personnel to diagnose and correct deficiencies.

The Fourth Edition of the ABCD Checklist

This new checklist is significantly more comprehensive than its predecessors. For this reason, we've organized the checklist into chapters based on basic business functions. These are:

- Strategic Planning Processes
- People/Team Processes
- Total Quality and Continuous Improvement Processes
- New Product Development Processes
- Planning and Control Processes

It would be an overwhelming task for most companies to attack simultaneously all of these business processes and their underlying technologies. Implementing all of these major changes at the same time would call for too much work to be done by people who already have full-time jobs in running the business.

There are significant risks in trying to do too much at one time: nothing gets done well, people burn out, and competitive advantage is lost.

The chapter organization of this checklist allows a company to choose one or several of these basic business processes and concentrate its energies on that choice. An organization can choose to pursue as much, or as little, as it feels capable of pursuing.

Qualitative Characteristics and Overview Items

Each chapter begins with brief Qualitative Characteristics of the various levels of performance—Class A, B, C, and D—for the processes in question. Then listed are the Overview Items, which provide an executive summary. They're designed to allow executives to evaluate whether necessary processes exist and, if so, how well they are being used.

Detail Items

Following this executive summary, the Detail Items are then spelled out, grouped under their respective Overview Items. These Detail Items provide additional information, guidance, and means for assessment, and make up the main body of the checklist. They're designed to provide operating managers with a tool for assessing the significant characteristics of each process, checking the vital "how tos" of each process, and analyzing in greater detail how well the processes are being used. For most of the Overview Items, several Detail Items are listed that will help determine your position on the scale for each Overview Item. A few Overview Items, however, have no Detail Items, and these are noted in the text with an asterisk (*).

Duplication of Entries

This checklist covers multiple technologies, and there's sometimes overlap from one to another. For example, many of the Overview and

Detail Items involved in effective People/Team Processes are necessary for Total Quality and Continuous Improvement Processes. Therefore, in some cases, it's been necessary to include the same items in more than one chapter. These have been noted in the text with a dagger (†).

Scoring of Responses

In prior editions of the checklist, responses were limited to "yes" or "no" (or, where appropriate, "not applicable").

This new checklist, however, enables responses to be made on a scale of 0 (Not Doing) to 4 (Excellent). This helps in identifying what's been done and what remains to be done, and can serve as an impetus for Continuous Improvement.

Objective

Our objective in publishing *The Oliver Wight ABCD Checklist for Operational Excellence* is to help companies become the best they can be. We hope you find this tool helps you to ask the right questions and determine the right answers to achieve absolute world-class performance, to become truly excellent in all operational aspects of the business. If so, then we have indeed produced a Class A product.

Walter E. Goddard
President
The Oliver Wight Companies

HOW TO USE THE CHECKLIST

The best way to use the checklist is as a vision of what could exist in your company, and pursue it aggressively, systematically, and relentlessly. Companies using the checklist in this way are using it effectively, and are achieving the potential of their organization.

Not all companies use the ABCD Checklist this way. Some companies use the checklist merely as a results indicator in the later stages of an implementation program. While beneficial, this does little to ensure continuing improvement.

For this reason, we recommend following the steps listed below to enable your company to use the checklist to achieve better results both in the short-term and on a sustained basis in the future.

Performance Improvement Process

1. Assess current status
2. Establish goals and objectives
3. Tailor the checklist to your company's immediate needs
4. Develop action plans
5. Measure progress
6. Conduct monthly management reviews

With the ABCD Checklist, the performance improvement process begins with an assessment of the company's current strengths and weaknesses. Many companies start by answering the questions that pertain to their areas of focus. If planning and control systems are an issue for your company, then you might focus only on this chapter. It's not necessary to answer the items in all five chapters. On the other hand, you may choose to address all five chapters to get an overall assessment of the situation in your company. However you choose to use the checklist, remember to answer *all* the questions in each chapter that you select. The only exception to this is when the items are not applicable to your business.

Most companies meet in groups of ten to twenty people to discuss the questions in the checklist. The groups allow for discussion and the comparing of differences. If one person feels the master production schedule is well managed but others can identify specific situations when poorly thought-out changes have been made, then a healthy discussion will take place. It's important to have several levels of management take part in these discussions, normally in several groups. It's typical for things to look better when viewed from the top of the organization.

There are a few prerequisites for these discussions to be useful. The first is that the participants must be knowledgeable. This means being familiar with the terms and techniques that are referenced and having an adequate understanding as to why the processes are important for the company to operate at a very high standard.

Second, it assumes that the answers will come from people of "good intentions." Knowledgeable people who are sincerely attempting to be objective can avoid seeing the world through rose-colored glasses or being overly critical to the extent that any minor imperfection leads to a negative response.

No matter how well phrased the items in this checklist may be, we recognize that degrees of interpretation are required to answer them. We also realize that a significant element of judgment is needed before answering many items. The combination of interpretation and judgment will, hopefully, lead to healthy internal discussion. The checklist will be productive if companies use it to review why these processes are important, what each process consists of, how the process can contribute to improvements, and how to accomplish these improvements.

Scoring the Results

The response to both Overview and Detail Items are scored on a range from "Excellent" to "Not Doing," with three intermediate points.

To determine where your performance falls on the range, use the following table as a guide.

Excellent *4 points*	Highest expected level of results from performing this activity.
Very Good *3 points*	Fully performing this activity and has achieved original goals associated with it.
Fair *2 points*	Has most of the processes, and tools are in place, but not fully utilizing the process and/or not getting the desired results.
Poor *1 point*	People, processes, data, and/or systems are not at the minimum prescribed level, resulting in little, if any, benefit.
Not Doing *0 points*	This activity is required but currently not being performed.

This method of scoring was chosen for the following reasons: It recognizes the work people have done, even though the company may not yet be at the "Excellent" level; it indicates where, and how much, additional work is required to achieve Class A results; it provides a means for Continuous Improvement—even at the Class A level, there is still room for improvement.

Most people answer the detail questions first, then use this information as a guide for answering the overview questions.

It's important to point out that the score for the overview questions is not an average of the scores for the detail questions. The detail questions are designed to help in determining the score for the overview question, but not all questions are of equal importance.

Calculating the Letter Grade

Once the Overview Items have been answered, complete the process of determining the letter grade for the chapter by averaging the numerical scores for the Overview Items.

- Average greater than 3.5 means that you are at the Class A level for that set of business processes.
- Average between 2.5 and 3.49 qualifies for Class B level.

- Average between 1.5 and 2.49 means Class C.
- Average less than 1.5 indicates a Class D level.

Moreover, before any company can be rated with confidence, there should be *at least three months of sustained performance*. As we all know, there are periods when everything appears to be working well, but it does not necessarily mean that the company has implemented the right set of tools or has learned to manage effectively using them. A single point in time is not sufficient to arrive at a firm conclusion.

Even a Class A rating in a particular set of business processes, however, should not be interpreted as achieving full utilization of your potential. A company achieving a Class A level of performance can still get better.

For example, if the company has achieved a Class A level of excellence in New Product Development Processes, there are obviously other business functions in which Class A can be attained. In addition, achieving Class A in New Product Development Processes doesn't mean there is no room for improvement, even in that area.

Many companies take pride in attaining a Class A level and then use this accomplishment as inspiration for further improvements. In fact, all of the companies who have attained the Class A level of performance tend to be very self-critical. They continue to see what remains, what can be done, and are aggressively pushing forward.

"I know we can get a lot better and must."

"The competition is tough, but so are we."

"The emphasis in our business is to give the customer what he wants, when he wants it, with continually lower lead times and excellent quality."

These are quotes from companies that are remarkably good today, but will be even better tomorrow.

Establish Goals and Objectives

The next critically important step is to establish the goals and objectives based on the assessment. These goals lead to accountabilities for the areas that need improvement. Someone (or several people) would be assigned the accountability for meeting the goals and objectives in the planned time frame for each task in the action plan.

To prevent backsliding in areas where the assessment has shown good results, one person (or several people) would be assigned the accountability for maintaining the current level of performance on each of these items.

Tailor Checklist to Your Company's Immediate Needs

Some companies tackle a number of areas for improvement simultaneously, while others go one step at a time. It used to be the norm that companies would start with one business function, for example, quality. Once they had made significant progress in that area, they would take on another initiative, perhaps Planning and Control Processes. Today the competitive pressures are such that many companies cannot afford to implement the new competitive tools one step at a time. Many companies are implementing several different business functions at once. For example, a number of companies have initiatives in progress on Planning and Control, Total Quality, and Continuous Improvement. Taking on this much work challenges a company's ability to manage change and puts significant strain on its resources. But the results are happening, and in less time than would be required if the different business functions were improved one at a time.

The new ABCD Checklist supports the implementation of one or many initiatives. You may choose to focus your implementation on one business function or several. When this implementation work is complete, one or more additional areas would be selected for implementation. By organizing the checklist into chapters, you can select one or several chapters to include in your current implementation plans.

In addition, we have created a data base version of the checklist for personal computers. The data base capabilities of this format allow a company to tailor the checklist to its implementation activities, creating a subset of the checklist containing the items being actively worked for improvement, and focusing attention on these items. In addition, the checklist software also includes a number of powerful tailoring and project management capabilities. These would be used to record the accountabilities, milestones, and target and actual performance levels for each item.

Develop Action Plans

With the goals established, the subset of activities defined, and the accountabilities in place, each person with specific accountabilities must now develop action plans for implementation. How are the goals to be achieved, what needs to be done to improve our ability to answer this question in the future, and what are the dates for completion and improvement? These are the questions that need to be answered in this phase of the improvement process.

Measure Progress

As progress is made, it should be recorded against the action plans created. Some questions can be measured quantitatively. For example, bill of material accuracy can be plotted, showing progress from the starting point to the agreed-upon goal. Other questions are more subjective, but still capable of measurement. An example would be surveying people's perceptions on top management's commitment to quality.

Conduct Monthly Management Reviews

Experience has shown it's important to conduct monthly reviews. The purpose is to monitor progress on currently active items and watch for slippage on established items. As with any implementation management review, the questions to ask are:

- Have the milestones been achieved?
- If not, what can be done to bring this aspect of the implementation back on schedule?
- What issues need to be resolved to continue our progress?

With these steps in mind as a method for improving the operational excellence of your organization, let's now look at the five chapters of the ABCD Checklist.

5

PLANNING AND CONTROL PROCESSES

QUALITATIVE CHARACTERISTICS

Class A   Planning and control processes are effectively used company wide, from top to bottom. Their use generates significant improvements in customer service, productivity, inventory, and costs.

Class B   These processes are supported by top management and used by middle management to achieve measurable company improvements.

Class C   Planning and control system is operated primarily as a better method for ordering materials; contributing to better inventory management.

Class D   Information provided by the planning and control system is inaccurate and poorly understood by users; providing little help in running the business.

OVERVIEW ITEMS

5-1 COMMITMENT TO EXCELLENCE

There is a commitment by top management and throughout the company to use effective planning and control techniques—providing a single set of numbers used by all members of the organization. These numbers represent valid schedules that people believe and use to run the business.

5-2 SALES AND OPERATIONS PLANNING

There is a sales and operations planning process in place that maintains a valid, current operating plan in support of customer requirements and the business plan. This process includes a formal meeting each month run by the general manager and covers a planning horizon adequate to plan resources effectively.

5-3 FINANCIAL PLANNING, REPORTING, AND MEASUREMENT

There is a single set of numbers used by all functions within the operating system, which provides the source data used for financial planning, reporting, and measurement.

5-4 "WHAT IF" SIMULATIONS

"What if" simulations are used to evaluate alternative operating plans and develop contingency plans for materials, people, equipment, and finances.

5-5 ACCOUNTABLE FORECASTING PROCESS

There is a process for forecasting all anticipated demands with suffi-cient detail and adequate planning horizon to support business planning, sales and operations planning, and master production scheduling. Forecast accuracy is measured in order to continuously improve the process.

5-6 SALES PLANS
There is a formal sales planning process in place with the sales force responsible and accountable for developing and executing the resulting sales plan. Differences between the sales plan and the forecast are reconciled.

5-7 INTEGRATED CUSTOMER ORDER ENTRY AND PROMISING
Customer order entry and promising are integrated with the master production scheduling system and inventory data. There are mechanisms for matching incoming orders to forecasts and for handling abnormal demands.

5-8 MASTER PRODUCTION SCHEDULING
The master production scheduling process is perpetually managed in order to ensure a balance of stability and responsiveness. The master production schedule is reconciled with the production plan resulting from the sales and operations planning process.

5-9 MATERIAL PLANNING AND CONTROL
There is a material planning process that maintains valid schedules and a material control process that communicates priorities through a manufacturing schedule, dispatch list, supplier schedule, and/or a kanban mechanism.

5-10 SUPPLIER PLANNING AND CONTROL
A supplier planning and scheduling process provides visibility for key items covering an adequate planning horizon.

5-11 CAPACITY PLANNING AND CONTROL
There is a capacity planning process using rough-cut capacity planning and, where applicable, capacity requirements planning in which planned capacity, based on demonstrated output, is balanced with required capacity. A capacity control process is used to measure and manage factory throughput and queues.

5-12 CUSTOMER SERVICE
An objective for on-time deliveries exists, and the customers are in agreement with it. Performance against the objective is measured.

5-13 SALES PLAN PERFORMANCE
Accountability for performance to the sales plan has been established, and the method of measurement and the goal has been agreed upon.

5-14 PRODUCTION PLAN PERFORMANCE
Accountability for production plan performance has been established, and the method of measurement and the goal has been agreed upon. Production plan performance is more than ± 2 percent of the monthly plan, except in cases where midmonth changes have been authorized by top management.

5-15 MASTER PRODUCTION SCHEDULE PERFORMANCE
Accountability for master production schedule performance has been established, and the method of measurement and the goal has been

agreed upon. Master production schedule performance is 95–100 percent of the plan.

5-16 MANUFACTURING SCHEDULE PERFORMANCE

Accountability for manufacturing schedule performance has been established, and the method of measurement and the goal has been agreed upon. Manufacturing schedule performance is 95–100 percent of the plan.

5-17 SUPPLIER DELIVERY PERFORMANCE

Accountability for supplier delivery performance has been established, and the method of measurement and the goal agreed upon. Supplier delivery performance is 95–100 percent of the plan.

5-18 BILL OF MATERIAL STRUCTURE AND ACCURACY

The planning and control process is supported by a properly structured, accurate, and integrated set of bills of material (formulas, recipes) and related data. Bill of material accuracy is in the 98–100 percent range.

5-19 INVENTORY RECORD ACCURACY

There is an inventory control process in place that provides accurate warehouse, stockroom, and work-in-process inventory data. At least 95 percent of all item inventory records match the physical counts, within the counting tolerance.

5-20 ROUTING ACCURACY

When routings are applicable, there is a development and maintenance process in place that provides accurate routing information. Routing accuracy is in the 95–100 percent range.

5-21 EDUCATION AND TRAINING†

An active education and training process for all employees is in place focused on business and customer issues and improvements. Its objectives include Continuous Improvement, enhancing the empowered worker, flexibility, employment stability, and meeting future needs.

5-22 DISTRIBUTION RESOURCE PLANNING (DRP)

Distribution Resource Planning, where applicable, is utilized to manage the logistics of distribution. DRP information is used for sales and operations planning, master production scheduling, supplier scheduling, transportation planning, and the scheduling of shipping.

OVERVIEW AND DETAIL ITEMS

5-1 COMMITMENT TO EXCELLENCE*

4—EXCELLENT 3—VERY GOOD 2—FAIR 1—POOR 0—NOT DOING

☐ ☐ ☐ ☐ ☐

There is a commitment by top management and throughout the company to use effective planning and control techniques—providing a single set of numbers used by all members of the organization. These numbers represent valid schedules that people believe and use to run the business.

5-2 SALES AND OPERATIONS PLANNING

☐ ☐ ☐ ☐ ☐

There is a sales and operations planning process in place that maintains a valid, current operating plan in support of customer requirements and the business plan. This process includes a formal meeting each month run by the general manager and covers a planning horizon adequate to plan resources effectively.

4—EXCELLENT 3—VERY GOOD 2—FAIR 1—POOR 0—NOT DOING

5-2a   There is a concise written sales and operations planning policy that covers the purpose, process, and participants in the process.

5-2b   Sales and operations planning is truly a process and not just a meeting. There is a sequence of steps that are laid out and followed.

5-2c   The meeting dates are set well ahead to avoid schedule conflicts. In case of an emergency and the department manager is unable to attend the meeting, he or she is represented by someone who is empowered to speak for the department.

5-2d   A formal agenda is circulated prior to the meeting.

5-2e   For each product family, plans are reviewed in units of measure that communicate most effectively.

5-2f   The new product development schedule is reviewed at the sales and operations planning meeting.

5-2g   All participants come prepared to the sales and operations planning meeting. There are preliminary meetings by department: Sales and Marketing to prepare a Sales Plan, Design Engineering to prepare a New Product Plan, Manufacturing to prepare a Production Plan.

4—EXCELLENT 3—VERY GOOD 2—FAIR 1—POOR 0—NOT DOING

5-2h   The presentation of information includes a review of both past performances and future plans for: sales, production, inventory, backlog, shipments, and new product activity.

☐ ☐ ☐ ☐ ☐

5-2i   Inventory and/or delivery lead time (backlog) strategies are reviewed each month as part of the process.

☐ ☐ ☐ ☐ ☐

5-2j   There is a process of reviewing and documenting assumptions about the business and the marketplace. This is to enhance the understanding of the business and represents the basis for future projections.

☐ ☐ ☐ ☐ ☐

5-2k   Sales and operations planning is an action process. Conflicts are resolved and decisions are made, communicated, and implemented.

☐ ☐ ☐ ☐ ☐

5-2l   Any large and/or unanticipated changes are communicated to other departments prior to the meeting in order to minimize surprises in the meeting.

☐ ☐ ☐ ☐ ☐

5-2m   Minutes of the meeting are circulated immediately after the meeting. This is typically done within twenty-four hours of the meeting.

☐ ☐ ☐ ☐ ☐

5-2n   The mechanism is in place to ensure that aggregate sales plans agree with detailed sales plans by item and by market segment or territory. There is a consensus from sales, marketing, and operating management.

☐ ☐ ☐ ☐ ☐

4—EXCELLENT 3—VERY GOOD 2—FAIR 1—POOR 0—NOT DOING

5-2o Time fences have been established as guidelines for managing changes. In the near-term, there is an effort to minimize the changes in order to gain the benefits of stability. In the mid-term range, priority changes are expected but are reviewed to ensure they can be executed. In the long-term, less precision is expected but direction is established.

5-2p Tolerances are established to determine acceptable performance for: sales, design engineering, finance, and production. They are reviewed and updated. Accountability is clearly established.

5-2q The master production schedules for a family of products are summed and checked for agreement with the production plan for that family. The sum of the master production schedules for a family of items is constrained by the production plan for that family.

5-2r There is an ongoing critique of the sales and operations planning process.

5-3 FINANCIAL PLANNING, REPORTING, AND MEASUREMENT
There is a single set of numbers used by all functions within the operating system, which provides the source data used for financial planning, reporting, and measurement.

4—EXCELLENT 3—VERY GOOD 2—FAIR 1—POOR 0—NOT DOING

5-3a   The financial projections developed in the sales and operations planning process are linked to the company's financial plans. When financial projections differ from the financial plans contained in the business plan, the differences are reconciled and either the sales and operations plan or the business plan is updated in order to measure performance.

☐ ☐ ☐ ☐ ☐

5-3b   The finance department uses the same source data as other departments for sales, shipments, and any other operating system information.

☐ ☐ ☐ ☐ ☐

5-3c   The finance department recognizes the limitations of traditional performance measurements, particularly those related to overhead allocation, and understands when and how those methods may produce misleading or incorrect data. Financial measurements, particularly those related to overhead allocation, have been reviewed and updated as necessary to support Just-in-Time practices.

☐ ☐ ☐ ☐ ☐

5-3d   All financial systems (billing, accounts payable, cost accounting, purchasing, receiving, inventory, etc.) are fully integrated with all transaction systems.

☐ ☐ ☐ ☐ ☐

5-3e   Accounts payable, purchasing, and receiving tie to material receipt transactions.

☐ ☐ ☐ ☐ ☐

4—EXCELLENT 3—VERY GOOD 2—FAIR 1—POOR 0—NOT DOING

5-3f   Labor reporting, either in the form of transactions or in the form of an allocation of labor hours, is used to determine the cost of the product.

□ □ □ □ □

5-3g   Where work orders are used, work order closing transactions are used to generate movement of inventory from one account to another in the general ledger and also to trigger variance reports for cost accounting purposes.

□ □ □ □ □

5-3h   Customer order shipment transactions drive the updating of finished goods inventory and the billing system at the same time.

□ □ □ □ □

5-3i   A cash-flow plan is prepared using the numbers from the operating system. The plan covers the sales and operation planning horizon, is reviewed at least monthly, and revised as changes occur.

□ □ □ □ □

5-3j   Simulation tools are actively used to convert operating data into financial data quickly for the purpose of simulation testing, decision making, and contingency planning.

□ □ □ □ □

5-3k   The finance department is proactive in simplifying all financial processes (e.g., cost accounting system) and eliminating nonvalue-added activities.

□ □ □ □ □

5-4 "WHAT IF" SIMULATIONS

*"What if" simulations are used to evaluate
alternative operating plans and develop
contingency plans for materials, people,
equipment, and finances.*

4—EXCELLENT 3—VERY GOOD 2—FAIR 1—POOR 0—NOT DOING

☐ ☐ ☐ ☐ ☐

5-4a   There is a computer-based simulation pro-   ☐ ☐ ☐ ☐ ☐
        cess supporting sales and operations plan-
        ning that permits the evaluation of various
        levels of demand, supply, production, in-
        ventory, and/or backlogs.

5-4b   There is a simulation capability used to   ☐ ☐ ☐ ☐ ☐
        support customer-order entry and promis-
        ing in determining the effects of making
        unplanned customer promises.

5-4c   Rough-cut capacity planning is used to   ☐ ☐ ☐ ☐ ☐
        evaluate the impact on critical resources of
        alternative production and master produc-
        tion schedule plans.

5-4d   Where applicable, capacity requirements   ☐ ☐ ☐ ☐ ☐
        planning is used to evaluate detailed ca-
        pacity constraints when planning and bud-
        geting labor and equipment needs.

5-4e   Where applicable, Material Requirements   ☐ ☐ ☐ ☐ ☐
        Planning and Distribution Requirements
        Planning are utilized to evaluate alternate
        planning factors (e.g., lot size, safety
        stock, lead time, etc.) and the resultant
        impact on inventory levels.

4—EXCELLENT 3—VERY GOOD 2—FAIR 1—POOR 0—NOT DOING
□ □ □ □ □

5-5 ACCOUNTABLE FORECASTING PROCESS

There is a process for forecasting all anticipated demands with sufficient detail and adequate planning horizon to support business planning, sales and operations planning, and master production scheduling. Forecast accuracy is measured in order to continuously improve the process.

5-5a There is clear accountability for developing the forecast, and the importance of this effort is reflected in the organization and reporting relationship of the forecasting function.
□ □ □ □ □

5-5b The forecaster (frequently called the demand planner or manager) understands the product, the customer base, the marketplace, and the manufacturing system.
□ □ □ □ □

5-5c All demands are included in the forecast, e.g., spares, samples, internal use, etc.
□ □ □ □ □

5-5d Available statistical forecasting tools are utilized when and where applicable.
□ □ □ □ □

5-5e Spare parts and other lower-level demands are handled with a forecasting system and appropriate order-entry mechanism that introduces the demands at the right level in the detailed material planning process.
□ □ □ □ □

4—EXCELLENT 3—VERY GOOD 2—FAIR 1—POOR 0—NOT DOING

5-5f   Detailed forecasts are reconciled with aggregate forecasts and communicated to the master production scheduler and sales force.   □ □ □ □ □

5-5g   The significant assumptions underlying the forecast are documented. They are reviewed at least monthly and updated as market conditions change.   □ □ □ □ □

5-5h   The forecaster participates in the product management and product development processes, including product structuring.   □ □ □ □ □

5-5i   Both aggregate and detailed measurements of forecast accuracy are used to improve the process.   □ □ □ □ □

5-6 SALES PLANS   □ □ □ □ □

There is a formal sales planning process in place with the sales force responsible and accountable for developing and executing the resulting sales plan. Differences between the sales plan and the forecast are reconciled.

5-6a   The sales force understands the impact of sales planning on the company's ability to satisfy its customers.   □ □ □ □ □

5-6b   Actual sales are measured against sales plans. Measurements are broken down into sales responsibility areas.   □ □ □ □ □

4—EXCELLENT 3—VERY GOOD 2—FAIR 1—POOR 0—NOT DOING

5-6c   The sales planning process is designed in   ☐ ☐ ☐ ☐ ☐
such a way as to minimize the administrative impact for the sales force.

5-6d   The incentives of the sales compensation   ☐ ☐ ☐ ☐ ☐
system are effective and do not inject bias into the sales plan and forecast.

5-6e   Where applicable, the sales force is actively pursuing customer linking. The customer's planning systems are linked with the company's to provide visibility of future demands.   ☐ ☐ ☐ ☐ ☐

5-6f   Aggregate forecasts are reconciled with   ☐ ☐ ☐ ☐ ☐
the sales plan.

5-6g   Sales participates with marketing, forecasting, and manufacturing in a demand planning meeting to prepare for each sales and operations planning meeting. A system is in use to communicate customer intelligence information to forecasting.   ☐ ☐ ☐ ☐ ☐

5-6h   Sales areas are provided with useful feedback regarding their performance to plan at least monthly. Sales plans are stated so that they are meaningful to the sales force yet translate into the sales and operations process.   ☐ ☐ ☐ ☐ ☐

5-6i   The assumptions underlying the sales plan   ☐ ☐ ☐ ☐ ☐
are documented. They are reviewed on a regular basis and changed as necessary.

5-7 INTEGRATED CUSTOMER ORDER ENTRY AND PROMISING

Customer order entry and promising are integrated with the master production scheduling system and inventory data. There are mechanisms for matching incoming orders to forecasts and for handling abnormal demands.

5-7a The order promising function has access to appropriate and timely information, such as Available-to-Promise (ATP), to ensure that good promises can be made. Where manufacturing times have been reduced such that production is based on actual customer orders, order promising would be based on the rate of production for the family of products. Otherwise, order promising would be based on the Available-to-Promise calculation for each item.

5-7b Sales and marketing participate in developing appropriate time fences for managing change.

5-7c There is a process in place for identifying and managing abnormal demands.

5-7d Abnormal demand (both active and history) is coded properly in the data base.

5-7e Customer orders are processed on a timely basis. The number of customer orders awaiting processing is measured and managed.

5-7f   Order-entry errors are measured and managed to eliminate the causes of the errors. □ □ □ □ □

5-7g   The number of customer-initiated sales change orders is measured and managed to an acceptable level. □ □ □ □ □

5-8 MASTER PRODUCTION SCHEDULING
□ □ □ □ □

The master production scheduling process is perpetually managed in order to ensure a balance of stability and responsiveness. The master production schedule is reconciled with the production plan resulting from the sales and operations planning process.

5-8a   Accountability for maintaining the master schedule is clear. The importance of master scheduling is reflected in the organization and reporting relationship of the master scheduling function. □ □ □ □ □

5-8b   The master scheduler understands the product, manufacturing process, manufacturing planning and control system, and the needs of the marketplace. □ □ □ □ □

5-8c   The master scheduler participates in and provides important detail information to the sales and operations planning process. □ □ □ □ □

5-8d   The master scheduler responds to feedback that identifies master schedule impacting material and/or capacity availability problems by initiating the problem-resolution process. □ □ □ □ □

4—EXCELLENT 3—VERY GOOD 2—FAIR 1—POOR 0—NOT DOING

5-8e   Planning bills of material (if used) are ☐ ☐ ☐ ☐ ☐
        maintained jointly by the master scheduler
        and sales and marketing.

5-8f   A written master schedule policy is fol- ☐ ☐ ☐ ☐ ☐
        lowed to monitor stability and responsive-
        ness; goals are established and measured.

5-8g   The master schedule is "firmed up" over a ☐ ☐ ☐ ☐ ☐
        sufficient horizon to enable stability of op-
        erations. Guidelines for this firmed hori-
        zon include:

        1. cumulative material lead time
        2. lead time to planned capacity
        3. lead time to cover customer order back-
           log (order book)

5-8h   Master schedule changes within the "firm ☐ ☐ ☐ ☐ ☐
        zone" (closest time fence) are managed;
        they are authorized by the appropriate
        people, measured, and reviewed for cause.

5-8i   Policy governs the use of safety stock and/ ☐ ☐ ☐ ☐ ☐
        or option overplanning used to increase
        responsiveness and compensate for incon-
        sistent supply and/or demand variations.

5-8j   The master schedule is summarized ap- ☐ ☐ ☐ ☐ ☐
        propriately and reconciled with the agreed
        to production rate (production plan) from
        the sales and operations planning process.

5-8k   All levels of master scheduled items are ☐ ☐ ☐ ☐ ☐
        identified and master scheduled.

4—EXCELLENT 3—VERY GOOD 2—FAIR 1—POOR 0—NOT DOING

5-8l   The master schedule is in weekly, daily, or □ □ □ □ □
smaller periods, may be rate-based, and
replanned at least weekly.

5-8m   The structure of the bills of material sup- □ □ □ □ □
ports the master scheduling/forecasting
process.

5-8n   Forecast consumption processes are used □ □ □ □ □
to prevent planning nervousness.

5-8o   The alternative approaches used with □ □ □ □ □
planning bills of material to develop production forecasts for master scheduled
items are well understood and an appropriate process is used.

5-8p   Rough-cut capacity planning, or its equiv- □ □ □ □ □
alent, is used to evaluate the impact of
significant master schedule changes on
critical resources. Demonstrated capacity
is measured and compared to required capacity.

5-8q   A finishing/final assembly mechanism or □ □ □ □ □
kanban approach is coordinated with the
master schedule to schedule customer orders to completion or replenish finished
goods.

5-8r   Where applicable, mixed-model master □ □ □ □ □
scheduling is being used.

5-8s   A weekly master schedule communica- □ □ □ □ □
tions meeting exists and is attended by all
using functions.

4—EXCELLENT 3—VERY GOOD 2—FAIR 1—POOR 0—NOT DOING

5-8t The linearity of output is measured; the graphic illustration of results should reflect daily performance to a planned linear output; reasons for deviations are highlighted with appropriate analysis.

☐ ☐ ☐ ☐ ☐

5-9 MATERIAL PLANNING AND CONTROL

☐ ☐ ☐ ☐ ☐

There is a material planning process that maintains valid schedules and a material control process that communicates priorities through a manufacturing schedule, dispatch list, supplier schedule, and/or a kanban mechanism.

Material Planning and Material Control

5-9a Material planners and schedulers understand the product, the manufacturing process, the manufacturing planning and control system, and are accountable for maintaining a valid plan.

☐ ☐ ☐ ☐ ☐

5-9b All involved employees—including planners, production people, buyers, etc.—operate under the "silence is approval" principle and are responsible to feed back schedule problems that cannot be resolved.

☐ ☐ ☐ ☐ ☐

5-9c   Planners are responsible for maintaining, periodically reviewing, and analyzing the accuracy and validity of all appropriate planning parameters such as order quantities or lot sizes, lead times, queues, safety stocks, etc.

5-9d   Production supervisors and buyers understand and use the system and are accountable for maintaining data integrity on information under their responsibility (e.g., point-of-use inventory, planning parameters and schedule, or order file data, etc.).

5-9e   There are formal communication processes among planning, production, and purchasing for the purpose of exchanging the information needed to maintain a valid schedule. The frequency and format (meetings, reports, calls) is determined by the situation.

5-9f   The informal priority systems (shortage list, hot list, priority codes, etc.) have been eliminated, and there is only one priority setting mechanism.

5-9g   MRP time periods are weekly or smaller to provide appropriate resolution of priorities.

5-9h   The MRP system is run as frequently as required to maintain valid schedules. Daily may be required, but weekly processing is a minimum.

4—EXCELLENT 3—VERY GOOD 2—FAIR 1—POOR 0—NOT DOING

5-9i The system uses standard logic to generate action/exception messages, including Need to Release Order, Need to Reschedule Order, Need to Cancel Order, Due Date, Past Due, or Release Past Due. ☐ ☐ ☐ ☐ ☐

5-9j The system has a firm planned order capability that is used, when necessary, to override the suggested plan. ☐ ☐ ☐ ☐ ☐

5-9k In reconciling problems, the planners bottom-up replan using single-level pegging to identify the source of demand. ☐ ☐ ☐ ☐ ☐

5-9l The system has an effective component availability checking mechanism and the planners use it to determine the feasibility of releasing an order or schedule. ☐ ☐ ☐ ☐ ☐

5-9m When applicable, the system includes the capability to alter the bill of material for an individual order when necessary to handle temporary substitutions, etc. ☐ ☐ ☐ ☐ ☐

5-9n All action/exception messages are prioritized, reviewed, and problems are acted upon in a timely manner. ☐ ☐ ☐ ☐ ☐

5-9o The number of action/exception messages for each planner is monitored for activity and trends. ☐ ☐ ☐ ☐ ☐

5-9p Where work orders are used, the volume of reschedules is tracked to monitor the stability of the plan and to determine the causes of excessive rescheduling activity. ☐ ☐ ☐ ☐ ☐

4—EXCELLENT 3—VERY GOOD 2—FAIR 1—POOR 0—NOT DOING

5-9q Where work orders are used, orders ☐ ☐ ☐ ☐ ☐
are released with full material availability
and full lead time 95–100 percent of the
time.

Shop Floor Control (where applicable)

5-9r Production management is accountable to ☐ ☐ ☐ ☐ ☐
meet operation due dates.

5-9s The dispatch list is the only priority tool, ☐ ☐ ☐ ☐ ☐
and operation due and start dates are the
only priority techniques used.

5-9t The system includes a detailed scheduling ☐ ☐ ☐ ☐ ☐
capability to create start and due dates
on a work order and operations within a
routing.

5-9u The system includes the capability to ☐ ☐ ☐ ☐ ☐
modify all start and due dates on a work
order and operations within a routing.

5-9v The system includes the capability to re- ☐ ☐ ☐ ☐ ☐
port status by operation.

5-9w An anticipated-delay reporting process is ☐ ☐ ☐ ☐ ☐
used to maintain due date validity.

5-9x The system includes a dispatch list by ☐ ☐ ☐ ☐ ☐
work center that shows item number, order
number, order quantity, operation number,
operation start and due date, and order
due date.

4—EXCELLENT 3—VERY GOOD 2—FAIR 1—POOR 0—NOT DOING

☐ ☐ ☐ ☐ ☐

5-10 SUPPLIER PLANNING AND CONTROL

A supplier planning and scheduling process provides visibility for key items covering an adequate planning horizon.

5-10a At least 80 percent of the suppliers have been educated in MRP II and/or JIT and understand the supplier scheduling process.

☐ ☐ ☐ ☐ ☐

5-10b Suppliers agree to plan raw material and capacity to meet the requirements displayed on the supplier schedule.

☐ ☐ ☐ ☐ ☐

5-10c There is a clear policy statement of the respective responsibilities of the supplier scheduler and buyer, including at what point each becomes involved in problem resolution.

☐ ☐ ☐ ☐ ☐

5-10d The supplier schedule displays planned orders and/or scheduled receipts over the planning horizon for all items provided by the supplier.

☐ ☐ ☐ ☐ ☐

5-10e Commitment zones are established in the supplier schedule representing firm commitments, material commitments, and capacity planning commitments.

☐ ☐ ☐ ☐ ☐

5-10f Time periods on the supplier schedule are weeks or smaller for at least the first four weeks displayed.

☐ ☐ ☐ ☐ ☐

4—EXCELLENT 3—VERY GOOD 2—FAIR 1—POOR 0—NOT DOING

5-10g The supplier scheduler and/or buyers meet with production planners as frequently as required to maintain a valid schedule. ☐ ☐ ☐ ☐ ☐

5-10h The suppliers understand the principle behind "silence is approval" and agree to notify the buyer in advance if a due date will be missed. ☐ ☐ ☐ ☐ ☐

5-10i Supplier schedules are communicated to suppliers at least weekly. ☐ ☐ ☐ ☐ ☐

5-10j For nonsupplier schedule items, 95 percent of purchase orders are released with full lead time. ☐ ☐ ☐ ☐ ☐

5-10k There is a purchasing policy that states the set of criteria that defines "key" items, which are planned and scheduled through a supplier scheduling process. Typical considerations include factors such as 80 percent of purchase content, long lead times, critical items, etc. ☐ ☐ ☐ ☐ ☐

5-11 CAPACITY PLANNING AND CONTROL

☐ ☐ ☐ ☐ ☐

There is a capacity planning process using rough-cut capacity planning and, where applicable, capacity requirements planning in which planned capacity, based on demonstrated output, is balanced with required capacity. A capacity control process is used to measure and manage factory throughput and queues.

Capacity Planning and Capacity Control

4—EXCELLENT 3—VERY GOOD 2—FAIR 1—POOR 0—NOT DOING

5-11a Capacity planning is well understood by all appropriate personnel and used to plan labor and machinery requirements.

☐ ☐ ☐ ☐ ☐

5-11b There is an understanding of the respective responsibilities of the capacity planner and production supervisor in the capacity management process (e.g., accountability for maintaining the accuracy of production-oriented capacity planning parameters such as planned capacity, number of workers and/or machines, number of shifts).

☐ ☐ ☐ ☐ ☐

5-11c Production supervisors and capacity planners meet at least weekly to resolve capacity issues.

☐ ☐ ☐ ☐ ☐

5-11d All activities that consume capacity are considered in developing the capacity requirement (e.g., maintenance, engineering projects, customized parts, etc.).

☐ ☐ ☐ ☐ ☐

5-11e Where applicable, other constraints such as engineering and supplier capacity are considered in the capacity management process.

☐ ☐ ☐ ☐ ☐

5-11f Work centers are appropriately defined to enable control of priorities and capacities while minimizing data maintenance, transactions, and reports.

☐ ☐ ☐ ☐ ☐

5-11g A "Load Factor" that recognizes capacity loss due to utilization, efficiency, and absenteeism is maintained and used in projecting capacity.

☐ ☐ ☐ ☐ ☐

4—EXCELLENT 3—VERY GOOD 2—FAIR 1—POOR 0—NOT DOING

5-11h Corrective action is taken to address over-
due capacity requirements caused by past
due orders.

☐ ☐ ☐ ☐ ☐

5-11i The capacity planning process includes
appropriate productivity analysis.

☐ ☐ ☐ ☐ ☐

Capacity Requirements Planning (where applicable)

5-11j System produces capacity requirements
summary report by work center and a detailed capacity report.

☐ ☐ ☐ ☐ ☐

5-11k Data used by the capacity planning system
is audited for accuracy. This includes capacity planning parameters such as demonstrated capacity, planned capacity (both
with reasonable tolerance), number of
workers/machines, number of shifts, number of hours per shift, etc.

☐ ☐ ☐ ☐ ☐

5-11l Process includes variance analysis of
planned and actual input, output, and
queue levels (Input/Output Report).

☐ ☐ ☐ ☐ ☐

The following items are key performance measurements of planning and control processes. See Appendix A for the preferred method of calculating the following performance measurements; see Appendix B for supplemental measurements.

5-12 CUSTOMER SERVICE

An objective for on-time deliveries exists, and the customers are in agreement with it. Performance against the objective is measured.

5-12a   Delivery to first promise and/or line item fill rate is at least 95 percent; higher is required by the customers.

5-12b   Graphs or charts showing the distribution of shipments about the promised date (target date) are maintained along with appropriate analysis, highlighting the primary causes of deviation.

5-13 SALES PLAN PERFORMANCE*

Accountability for performance to the sales plan has been established, and the method of measurement and the goal has been agreed upon.

5-14 PRODUCTION PLAN PERFORMANCE*

Accountability for production plan performance has been established, and the method of measurement and the goal has been agreed upon. Production plan performance is more than ±2 percent of the monthly plan, except in cases where midmonth changes have been authorized by top management.

4—EXCELLENT 3—VERY GOOD 2—FAIR 1—POOR 0—NOT DOING

5-15 MASTER PRODUCTION SCHEDULE PERFORMANCE*

□ □ □ □ □

Accountability for master production schedule performance has been established, and the method of measurement and the goal has been agreed upon. Master production schedule performance is 95–100 percent of the plan.

5-16 MANUFACTURING SCHEDULE PERFORMANCE*

□ □ □ □ □

Accountability for manufacturing schedule performance has been established, and the method of measurement and the goal has been agreed upon. Manufacturing schedule performance is 95–100 percent of the plan.

5-17 SUPPLIER DELIVERY PERFORMANCE*

□ □ □ □ □

Accountability for supplier delivery performance has been established, and the method of measurement and the goal agreed upon. Supplier delivery performance is 95–100 percent of the plan.

5-18 BILL OF MATERIAL STRUCTURE AND ACCURACY

□ □ □ □ □

The planning and control process is supported by a properly structured, accurate, and integrated set of bills of material (formulas, recipes) and related data. Bill of material accuracy is in the 98–100 percent range.

5-18a Responsibility and accountability for developing and maintaining bills of material are clearly defined in written policy.

5-18b All functions that use the bills of materials participate in their structuring.

5-18c Bills of material are properly structured, represent the way products are built, and support the planning and control processes.

5-18d There is a bill of material accuracy audit process in place. This process examines the bill of material at a single level, looking for correct components, quantity per, and component unit of measure.

5-18e Audit results show the bills of material to be in the 98–100 percent range.

5-18f Finance uses the bill of material in costing the product.

5-18g There is a policy and procedure in place that identifies who is responsible for loading and maintaining each field of the item master file.

5-19 INVENTORY RECORD ACCURACY
There is an inventory control process in place that provides accurate warehouse, stockroom, and work-in-process inventory data. At least 95 percent of all item inventory records match the physical counts, within the counting tolerance.

5-19a Accountability for maintaining accurate inventory records is clearly understood by all those controlling inventories. This includes raw materials, finished goods, work-in-process, and point-of-use inventory. ☐ ☐ ☐ ☐ ☐

5-19b Cycle counting procedures are used to identify and resolve inventory errors and measure inventory accuracy. ☐ ☐ ☐ ☐ ☐

5-19c The cycle counting process has replaced the periodic physical inventory. ☐ ☐ ☐ ☐ ☐

5-19d Cycle count results show the inventory records to be in the 95–100 percent range. ☐ ☐ ☐ ☐ ☐

5-20 ROUTING ACCURACY ☐ ☐ ☐ ☐ ☐
When routings are applicable, there is a development and maintenance process in place that provides accurate routing information. Routing accuracy is in the 95–100 percent range.

5-20a There is a written policy that clearly identifies responsibility and accountability for developing and maintaining routings. ☐ ☐ ☐ ☐ ☐

5-20b All functions that use the routings participate in their development. ☐ ☐ ☐ ☐ ☐

5-20c The routings represent the way products are made and are integrated with the bills of materials. ☐ ☐ ☐ ☐ ☐

4—EXCELLENT
3—VERY GOOD
2—FAIR
1—POOR
0—NOT DOING

5-20d   There is a routing accuracy audit process ☐ ☐ ☐ ☐ ☐
in place. This process examines the rout-
ings for proper sequence of operations,
work center number, missing or unnecessary operations, and, with tolerance,
set-up and run times.

5-20e   Audit results show the routings to be in the ☐ ☐ ☐ ☐ ☐
95–100 percent range.

5-20f   Finance uses the routing in costing the ☐ ☐ ☐ ☐ ☐
product.

5-21 EDUCATION AND TRAINING† ☐ ☐ ☐ ☐ ☐
*An active education and training process for all
employees is in place focused on business and
customer issues and improvements. Its objectives
include Continuous Improvement, enhancing the
empowered worker, flexibility, employment
stability, and meeting future needs.*

5-21a   Management attitude and actions demon- ☐ ☐ ☐ ☐ ☐
strate a commitment to fully educate and
train people prior to implementation of
new technologies and processes.

5-21b   Education is a participative process rather ☐ ☐ ☐ ☐ ☐
than a one-directional flow from the top of
the organization to the bottom.

5-21c   The education and training process recog- ☐ ☐ ☐ ☐ ☐
nizes people at all levels as experts in their
areas, communicates objectives, and fully
involves people in the process of changing
their jobs.

5-21d The education and training approach is based on the principles of behavior change in an organization rather than merely a process of fact transfer regarding a specific technology.

5-21e The company has committed sufficient resources, financial and otherwise, to education and training.

5-21f An ongoing education and training process is used to refine and improve the use of business tools like team-based technologies, Just-in-Time (JIT), Total Quality Control (TQC), Manufacturing Resource Planning system (MRP II), etc.

5-21g Areas of employee improvement needs are continuously assessed.

5-22 DISTRIBUTION RESOURCE PLANNING (DRP)

Distribution Resource Planning, where applicable, is utilized to manage the logistics of distribution. DRP information is used for sales and operations planning, master production scheduling, supplier scheduling, transportation planning, and the scheduling of shipping.

5-22a There is a concise written Distribution Resource Planning policy that covers purpose, process, and participants.

5-22b   Distribution requirements are considered and reconciled through the sales and operations planning and master production scheduling processes. □ □ □ □ □

5-22c   The distribution network maintained in the DRP system is complete; it reflects which items are stocked at each distribution center. □ □ □ □ □

5-22d   Forecasts are available for each stock-keeping unit in each distribution center. □ □ □ □ □

5-22e   Time periods for DRP are weeks or smaller. □ □ □ □ □

5-22f   Distribution Resource Planning is run weekly or more frequently. □ □ □ □ □

5-22g   The DRP system includes the following characteristics: □ □ □ □ □

1. firm planned orders
2. pegging capabilities
3. customer orders promised for future deliveries in addition to forecasts
4. the ability to include backorders in the netting logic
5. the ability to maintain and change inventory records, location records, and scheduled receipts
6. supplier scheduling in order to provide adequate visibility to outside suppliers
7. rescheduling messages

4—EXCELLENT 3—VERY GOOD 2—FAIR 1—POOR 0—NOT DOING

5-22h The system provides pertinent information for transportation planning in order to be responsive to the needs of the distribution centers as well as to reduce transportation costs.

□ □ □ □ □

5-22i The system provides a shipping schedule that enables cost reductions while at the same time satisfying established loading and shipping needs.

□ □ □ □ □

5-22j Kanban may be used to trigger replenishment from the central supply facility to the distribution centers.

□ □ □ □ □